TWO MINUTES
IN THE **BIBLE**™

THROUGH
Proverbs

ᗢᗢᗡ

BOYD BAILEY

HARVEST HOUSE PUBLISHERS
EUGENE, OREGON

Cover by Left Coast Design, Portland, Oregon

Cover photo © boscorelli / Shutterstock

TWO MINUTES IN THE BIBLE is a trademark of Boyd Bailey. Harvest House Publishers, Inc., is the exclusive licensee of the trademark TWO MINUTES IN THE BIBLE.

TWO MINUTES IN THE BIBLE™ THROUGH PROVERBS
Copyright © 2015 Boyd Bailey
Published by Harvest House Publishers
Eugene, Oregon 97402
www.harvesthousepublishers.com

Library of Congress Cataloging-in-Publication Data
    Bailey, Boyd, 1960-
    Two minutes in the Bible through Proverbs / Boyd Bailey.
        pages cm
    ISBN 978-0-7369-6530-9 (pbk.)
    ISBN 978-0-7369-6531-6 (eBook)
    1. Bible. Proverbs—Meditations. I. Title.
    BS1465.54.B35 2015
    242'.5—dc23

                                                                    2014049503

Printed in the United States of America

16 17 18 19 20 21 22 23 / VP-CD / 10 9 8 7 6 5

To Andy Stanley
My friend, my pastor, and the wisest person I know

Walk with the wise and become wise.
PROVERBS 13:20

Acknowledgments

Thank you, Rita, for asking me, "Is this the wise thing to do?"

Thank you, Rebekah, Rachel, Bethany, and Anna Grace, for being daughters who seek to make wise choices.

Thank you, JT, Tripp, and Todd, for being sons-in-law who walk with the wise!

Thank you, George Morgan, for a life that modeled daily meditation on the Proverbs.

Thank you, Donna Reed, Susan Fox, and Lee McCutchan, for your expert editing.

Thank you, Charlie and Patty Renfroe, for being mentors who exemplify wise decision making.

Thank you, Steve Reed, for instructing me in wisdom, especially the seven years we traveled together.

Thank you, Lanny Donoho, Mike Kendrick, Woody Faulk, and Joel Manby, for ten years of accountability in wise decision making.

Introduction

Wisdom is what every God-fearing person wants. The Lord has put in the heart of His disciples a desire to live with His perspective. Indeed, a heart of wisdom continues to grow as a follower of Jesus seeks to know Him and understand His Word. Hunting for wisdom is a process of humble learning that lasts a lifetime. The wise never arrive in their acquisition of God's knowledge, wisdom, and principles for living. Students continue seeking wisdom.

When I was 31 years old, a friend described to me his wisdom journey. I listened intently because his life was worth emulating. He was the spiritual leader of his family, a respected businessman, and a student of the Scriptures. Astonishingly, for ten years he daily read a chapter in Proverbs based on the day of the month. For example, on May 3 he read Proverbs 3 and meditated on its meaning for his life.

I felt the Holy Spirit prompting me to accept that same challenge, so from age 31 to age 41, each day I read the chapter in Proverbs that corresponded with the day of the month. The lessons I learned mirrored my life experiences so often, it was uncanny. Everything I gleaned, from the wise management of money to avoiding sexual temptation, transformed my behavior. Ideas about parenting, marriage, and relationships motivated me to serve others selflessly.

When we apply the principles of Proverbs to our lives, we are changed. If we humbly and consistently follow these extremely practical teachings, we grow in Christ's character. Once the Holy Spirit illumines our mind to understand the enormous benefit of living out the Lord's principles, we become responsible to embed them in our behavior. Knowledge without application results in lifeless pseudo spirituality.

So we struggle together to be consistent with honest speech, kind attitudes, humble service, and sharing the truth in love. Like an athlete in training, we work hard at developing godly habits. The process is painful and frustrating at times, but we stay the course of character development for Christ's sake. Proverbs applied produce the fruit of faith.

I am grateful that Solomon, the instrument God's Spirit used to pen these inspired and inerrant words, was a work in progress himself. He did not always practice what he preached, and he suffered because of his foolish decisions. But he was wise to come back to the baseline of belief in the ways of the Lord as the best course for living. You and I will stumble along the way, and our actions will be inconsistent, but we are wise to regularly recalibrate for Christ.

Are you looking to love the Lord and people with authenticity? Do you want to be a leader worth following, a father who is admired, a mother who is appreciated, a child who is pleasant, a disciple of Jesus who is growing in grace? If so, then seek to know God's heart on how to live life, which He beautifully lays out in the principles of Proverbs.

The book of Proverbs is not like a magic wand that we use to make every difficult situation simply disappear, but it is a guide that shapes our thoughts, prayers, and experiences. Follow Jesus as He reveals His ways in these wise and ancient words that have proven true for more than 3000 years. Wisdom has a track record of bolstering our trust in God, love for God, and fear of God. Be wise!

1

Keep Learning

⸺⸺⸺⸺ ∞∞∞ ⸺⸺⸺⸺

Let the wise listen and add to their learning,
and let the discerning get guidance.

Proverbs 1:5

Wise men and women are lifelong learners. The knowledge and understanding that served us well last year will not be sufficient for following years. The lessons we are learning today are preparing us for tomorrow. Wise and discerning people listen and learn. They listen to people around them and learn what to do and what not to do.

Another person's tragedy can warn us of decisions to avoid. When you see a family destroyed by debt, you learn the discipline of saving. On the other hand, another person's triumph can teach us to embrace good choices. The sacrifice of a mom who stays home to serve her family increases the probability of children with character. Listen to her life and learn how to teach little ones to love Jesus. Always keep learning.

⸺⸺ ∞∞∞ ⸺⸺

Instruct the wise and they will be wiser still;
teach the righteous and they will add
to their learning (Proverbs 9:9).

Your counsel increases in value as you grow in wisdom and discernment. Lazy learners tend to be ignored. Others desire to learn from an educated life, so seek out a mentor who models learning. Meet weekly with this person, and invite him or her to challenge your assumptions and question your answers more than answer your questions. Oral learning through the exchange of ideas unlocks and applies wisdom. You are positioned to learn in an audience of one with graying hair.

Above all, learn by submission to God and His Word. A humble life can be trusted with God's wisdom and the Holy Spirit's discernment. As you live a life of compassion and mercy, your knowledge will be converted to wisdom. Keep learning, and the Lord will lift you to new levels of influence. Stop learning, and you will sink into irrelevance. Learning expands your kingdom effectiveness and deepens your character.

———∞∞∞———

The LORD gives wisdom;
from his mouth come knowledge and
understanding (Proverbs 2:6).

What lesson do I need to learn today so I can better serve the Lord and others tomorrow?

Related Readings
Deuteronomy 5:1; 31:13; Job 34:2-4; Psalm 119:73; Hebrews 5:8

2

Listen to Your Parents

―――――∞∞――――――

Listen, my son, to your father's instruction
and do not forsake your mother's teaching.

Proverbs 1:8

Parents are God's provision for protection and learning. Therefore, as we listen to them, we can learn from God. We learn lessons on living frugally, being honest, and working hard. We also learn what not to do, such as eating poorly, not exercising, and not forgiving. Parents teach and children learn regardless of whether either recognizes the educational exchange. This learning process is meant to help each generation improve.

Parental honor is the cornerstone of any family that is forging their faith in Christ. Without learning from your parents' mistakes and building on their successes, you are destined to dysfunction. You honor your parents when you listen to them, learn from them, and obey them. You honor God as you honor your mom and dad, so value your parents because of their position rather than their performance.

―――――∞∞――――――

Children, obey your parents in the Lord, for this
is right. "Honor your father and mother"―which
is the first commandment with a promise―"so
that it may go well with you and that you may
enjoy long life on the earth" (Ephesians 6:1-3).

This high honor and esteem of parents helps entire nations of families to focus on what makes a lasting legacy. Once a society sequesters the elderly in isolation as a burden and offers euthanasia as an option, the beginning of the end of that foolish culture has arrived. As we serve our parents, we will see Jesus. They can provide perspective only experience affords.

Take the time to look past the rough exterior of your dad and determine to draw out his nuggets of wisdom. Help your mom process her fears and forgive her shortcomings, and you will see the beauty of her advice. Parents are not perfect, but even in their imperfection they invite honor and attention. Listen to your parents and learn from them, and you will learn from the Lord. Parents are a gift from God, so receive them by faith and steward the relationship in humility and love.

You know the commandments: "You shall not commit adultery, you shall not murder, you shall not steal, you shall not give false testimony, honor your father and mother" (Luke 18:20).

Into what area of my life will I invite my parents' advice and feedback in an honorable way?

Related Readings
Genesis 49:2; Exodus 18:24; Proverbs 23:22; 1 Timothy 5:4

3

Stand Alone

My son, do not go along with them,
do not set foot on their paths;
for their feet rush into evil,
they are swift to shed blood.

Proverbs 1:15-16

S tand against the shameful ways of sinful men and women, even if you have to stand alone. If no one else speaks up, your Savior stands with you in your seclusion. It is more convenient to compromise your convictions, but find strength in what God says and obey it. If you have to stand alone for a season, your perseverance in doing what is right will eventually prod others to follow your example.

Avoid the bar and unseemly clubs on business trips, and others will find the courage to join you. At college, pray instead of party, study instead of steal, serve instead of acting silly, and be faithful instead of foolish. Young adults are longing for reliable friends and communities of trust, learning, and accountability. Stand alone and see God work wonders.

If I do judge, my decisions are true, because I am not
alone. I stand with the Father, who sent me (John 8:16).

To step into a seductive snare of sin is foolish. When you see it coming, do not go there, or you will be like a silly bird whose curiosity leads it into a trap. The pain that results from not standing alone in the truth is reason enough to remain in the character of Christ. However, there are other benefits. You stand alone so your compelling story of courage inspires your children now and as they grow older. You stand alone so you can look your spouse in the eyes and honestly say you value him or her much more than any other. You stand alone so the people you serve grow in confidence that you have their very best interest in mind. Most importantly, you stand alone by the grace of God in humility and faith.

Don't become proud of standing alone, or you will fall—suddenly and severely. Rather, stand alone by staying on your knees in desperate dependence on God. Give Him the glory, and He will give you the gumption to go it alone when necessary.

> The one whose walk is blameless,
>   who does what is righteous,
>   who speaks the truth from their heart…
>   Whoever does these things will never
>   be shaken (Psalm 15:2,5).

Where do I need to stand alone as an encouragement to those who may be holding back for fear of what others might think or do?

Related Readings

Job 23:13; Proverbs 12:7; Luke 21:19; 1 Corinthians 10:12

4

The Knowledge of God

*If you look for [wisdom] as for silver
and search for it as for hidden treasure,
then you will understand the fear of the LORD
and find the knowledge of God.*

Proverbs 2:4-5

The knowledge of God is obtained by the wisdom of God, and the wisdom of God is found in the Word of God. Jesus is the Word, so when we see Him, we see not only our Savior but also our God. Jesus became flesh and walked among us so He could, among other things, teach us the knowledge of God. So read the four Gospels. You will observe the knowledge of God lived out in your Lord.

You will learn obedience by understanding and applying His teachings. Obtaining the knowledge of God and integrating it into your life are not passive exercises. Transformation occurs through passionate prayer as you earnestly seek to understand Jesus's words and actions. Knowledge of God is food that satisfies the soul. It is a divine diet of grace and truth.

Like newborn babies, long for the pure milk
of the word, so that by it you may grow in
respect to salvation (1 Peter 2:2 NASB).

You read and receive the Word of God so you can be transformed by the knowledge of God. Wisdom is the way to knowing God. It is discovered through toil and trust, industry and intimacy, hard work and heaven's illumination. Just as if you were mining the precious metals of silver and gold, you will find the knowledge of God in the discipline and determination of digging out truth that may be covered over by the rubble of unbelief.

You rise up early so you can meditate in the mine shaft with your Master Jesus, and He shows you the way. As you humbly receive the knowledge of God, let others benefit from the richness of your discovery. Invest wisdom in others for the sake of God's kingdom. You can begin by being a spiritual leader at work and home.

───⚬⚬⚬───

On the second day the heads of fathers' households
of all the people, the priests and the Levites were
gathered to Ezra the scribe that they might gain insight
into the words of the law (Nehemiah 8:13 NASB).

How can I use my knowledge of God to bless and encourage others?

Related Readings
Job 28:12,20,23; John 1:1-14; 2 Peter 1:5

5

The Marriage Covenant

Wisdom will save you also from the adulteress woman,
from the wayward wife with her seductive words,
who has left the partner of her youth
and ignored the covenant she made before God.

Proverbs 2:16-17

Marriage is a covenant before God, not to be messed with by man. Christian marriage is not a secular ceremony but a Christ-centered commitment "until death do us part." However, there are tempters, both men and women, who try to take away the trust between husbands and wives. Their lives are unhappy, so they scheme for artificial satisfaction at the expense of other people's marriages.

Sin is not passive but active, so be on prayerful alert not to listen to its allure. Pay attention and do not place yourself in compromising circumstances. Marriage is a sacred obligation. God is not only a witness but also the One who instituted the ordinance, so stay true to Him and to your true love.

Marriage should be honored by all, and the marriage
bed kept pure, for God will judge the adulterer
and all the sexually immoral (Hebrews 13:4).

Husbands and wives are accountable to each other under the authority of Almighty God. This is why wayward men and women suffer consequences when they disrespect the marriage vows. Disobedience to an oath before God can damage and destroy relationships, reputations, financial security, emotional stability, and physical health. Husbands and wives who take their commitment to Christ and each other seriously are not seduced into sex outside their marriage.

How do you maintain this high standard? By God's grace you romance each other as you did when you were dating. You share your heart and affections only with your true love, the husband or bride of your youth. You determine not to be alone with anyone of the opposite sex, as this can feed temptation. You celebrate and uphold marriage as a solemn covenant before the Lord, family, friends, and each other.

—⊶⊷—

> Thus says the Lord GOD, "As I live, surely My oath
> which he despised and My covenant which he
> broke, I will inflict on his head" (Ezekiel 17:19 NASB).

How can I honor my spouse by respecting our marriage as a covenant before God?

Related Readings
Numbers 5:12-22; Malachi 2:14-16; Matthew 5:27-32

6

Walking Wisely

*Thus you will walk in the ways of the good
and keep to the paths of the righteous.*

Proverbs 2:20

To walk wisely is to keep company with those who love and obey Christ. They are your influencers because their values lead you along the route you want to take in life. When people pray together on behalf of the greater good of God's kingdom, their purposes are aligned.

So in college, walk with the crowd who is all about character building, service to others, studies, love for the Lord, and obedience to His commands. At work, prayerfully partner with those who are principled in their business philosophy. Some people may have less skill and experience than you do, but you can trust their heart to do what they say they will do. Moreover, do not negotiate with mediocre living as it is distasteful in the mouth of your Master Jesus. Instead, walk with those who raise you to righteous living.

Walk with the wise and become wise,
for a companion of fools suffers harm
(Proverbs 13:20).

Of course, you are to reach out to sinners, care for them, and let your love lead them to the Lord. God has placed you in unbelievers' lives to influence them toward heaven. Perhaps one day they will thank you for your patience and prayers. But those who walk wisely also learn well by being with those who aspire to intimacy with the Almighty. They walk with the ones who obey the One.

As you become wise, make room for others who want to walk with you and learn from you. Your family may need you to slow down so they can benefit from your presence. Walk with your sons and daughters while you can. Your influence at work will grow when you walk with your team. Above all else, walk with the Lord, and He will show you whom to walk with and how.

───✦───

This is what the LORD says:
"Stand at the crossroads and look;
　　ask for the ancient paths,
ask where the good way is, and walk in it,
　　and you will find rest for your souls.
But you said, 'We will not walk in it'"
(Jeremiah 6:16).

With whom do I need to cease walking? With whom do I need to continue walking? And with whom do I need to begin walking?

Related Readings

Psalm 119:63-115; 1 Corinthians 5:11; Hebrews 6:12

7

Humble Wisdom

Do not be wise in your own eyes;
fear the LORD and shun evil.

Proverbs 3:7

Humble wisdom is the opposite of a holier-than-thou attitude. It is contrite before Christ and modest before men. Humble wisdom is grateful to God for His blessings of insight and understanding into eternal matters. Wisdom is not a badge of superiority to be worn with pride, but a blanket of security that humbles the heart.

Wisdom without humility leads to conceit and a condescending attitude. It is ugly and disfigures the soul. Consider star athletes who are so full of themselves, they fail to reach their potential for lack of team support. In contrast, humble wisdom says, "I am a fellow learner of the Lord's ways; I am a work in progress just like you." God entrusts His wisdom to humble hearts, so be desperate for divine direction.

Who is wise and understanding among you? Let
them show it by their good life, by deeds done in
the humility that comes from wisdom (James 3:13).

As wisdom increases in your heart and mind, pride must decrease. The fear of the Lord keeps you from thinking you can be anything special outside of your Savior Jesus. The fear of God does not forget that wisdom comes from above. Yes, your experience enhances wisdom, and your pain can lead to wisdom, but ultimately wisdom resides with God and His Word.

This is why in humility you hunker down and pray, "Heavenly Father, I bow in awe before You and ask for insight and direction. You are the author of all wisdom."

Submission to Christ and His commands squeezes out selfish, worldly wisdom and replaces it with the humble wisdom of heaven. Therefore, request wisdom for His glory and never cease to learn from those whom the Lord sends daily into your life.

Live in harmony with one another; do not be haughty (snobbish, high-minded, exclusive), but readily adjust yourself to [people, things] and give yourselves to humble tasks. Never overestimate yourself or be wise in your own conceits (Romans 12:16 AMP).

Whom can I learn from today to become wiser in humility of mind and heart?

Related Readings
1 Kings 3:4-15; Isaiah 5:21; Romans 1:20-25; Revelation 14:7

8

Honorable Wealth

꠾

Honor the LORD with your wealth,
with the firstfruits of all your crops;
then your barns will be filled to overflowing,
and your vats will brim over with new wine.

Proverbs 3:9-10

Why do we honor the Lord with our wealth? We honor Him because He is the giver of all good things, the author of our abundance. As our estate grows, so should our honor of our heavenly Father. Otherwise, we are tempted to take credit for our success, honoring ourselves. The Bible says, "You may say in your heart, 'My power and the strength of my hand made me this wealth'" (Deuteronomy 8:17 NASB).

In some seasons our net worth decreases, and we are reminded that Christ controls cash flow. Wealth is not an end to itself, but the means to the greater goal of honoring God. Peace and contentment flow from wealth that honors the Lord, while fear and insecurity consume the heart that honors itself. The psalmist warned, "If riches increase, do not set your heart upon them" (Psalm 62:10 NASB).

So how do you honor the Lord with your wealth? One way is to remain faithful and give Him the firstfruits of your fortune. Small or large as your gift may be, His primary concern is your faithfulness to give. You give out of obedience, not abundance. People see Christ when you keep your cash commitments, especially when it costs you. This is honorable in heaven and on earth. Give to your church, the poor and needy, widows, orphans, family, and ministries who align with your passions.

The result of your generous giving in the middle of downward financial pressure will be an upward blessing to you and the recipients. Your honorable use of wealth for Jesus's sake may mean food, clothing, shelter, and medical supplies for a village, or Bibles translated into the foreign tongue of a remote people halfway around the world. The best time to aggressively give is when the need is greatest. Take care to honor Christ with generous giving, and He will take care of you. What you give now, you will have in abundance later.

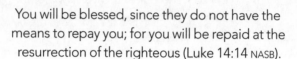

You will be blessed, since they do not have the
means to repay you; for you will be repaid at the
resurrection of the righteous (Luke 14:14 NASB).

How can I be honorable and remain faithful to my financial commitments to Christ?

Related Readings
Deuteronomy 26:1-15; Luke 12:15-32; 1 Corinthians 15:20; Philippians 4:17-19

9

Sweet Sleep

When you lie down, you will not be afraid;
when you lie down, your sleep will be sweet.

Proverbs 3:24

Sweet sleep comes to a secure soul. Wise is the one who lays his worries at the feet of Jesus before he lies down at night. Fear is foreign to those who sleep sweetly in the safe arms of their Savior. If you are a light sleeper, learn to listen to the Lord, write down what He is saying, and go back to bed. The Almighty may awaken you, as He did Samuel (see 1 Samuel 3), only to rock you back to sleep in a more restful place.

The Lord neither sleeps nor slumbers. He is a trustworthy sentinel, watching over you in your most vulnerable state. God is on guard, so you do not have to sit up and see what is going on. You can lie down by faith and wake up rested and refreshed. A good night's rest is a gift from God, ready for you to receive by faith. David, a man who faced many fears, confidently prayed, "In peace I will both lie down and sleep for You alone, O Lord, make me to dwell in safety" (Psalm 4:8 NASB).

Christ uses a clear conscience to calm your emotions, settle your mind, and create sweet sleep. If demons of guilt are engaged in your head, you will have a hard time sleeping. You can clear your conscience by humbly taking responsibility for your behavior and asking forgiveness from God and man for sinful attitudes and actions. Integrity and uprightness preserve you from pride and precarious living.

A clear conscience results from working through relational conflict. Why allow broken relationships to rob you of rest? Instead, go immediately in humility and initiate reconciliation. That will lead to rest as stress gives way to relational healing. Simply talking through tension with a teachable heart releases anxieties and fears. A clear conscience that keeps short accounts will benefit in sweet sleep.

> Therefore, if you are offering your gift at the altar
> and there remember that your brother or sister has
> something against you, leave your gift there in front
> of the altar. First go and be reconciled to them;
> then come and offer your gift (Matthew 5:23-24).

With whom do I need to seek reconciliation so we can both rest in sweet sleep?

Related Readings
Job 11:18; Psalm 121:4-7; Mark 4:38; Acts 12:6

10

Wise Guides

———— ∞∞∞ ————

I instruct you in the way of wisdom
and lead you along straight paths.

Proverbs 4:11

God places wise guides in our lives to lead us in the way of wisdom. These are men and women with a touch of gray or a head full of fine silver—and discernment. Their counsel is the cream that rises to the top of all the advice we receive. Their opinions are like a road map from our heavenly Father. Can you meet an hour or two weekly with these sages from your Savior? If you can, you will more clearly see the wise way to walk.

Life is full of circumstances that make your path crooked, but with wise guides and aggressive prayer, you can stay focused on the way of wisdom. Ask fellow wisdom hunters to pray that your heart will stay on the path of purity. The righteous prayers of the wise reveal the way with heaven's headlights, so request prayer often.

———— ∞∞∞ ————

By day the LORD went ahead of them in a pillar of
cloud to guide them on their way and by night
in a pillar of fire to give them light, so that they
could travel by day or night (Exodus 13:21).

Solicit the prayers of wise saints who seek the Lord daily in determined intercession. Ask them to pray for your heart, mind, and body to be kept clean in Christ Jesus. Entrust wise prayer warriors with specific financial and family issues that need a touch from heaven. Each of us needs to be surrounded by a prayer team—ambassadors to Almighty God on our behalf.

These trusted friends cooperate with you and Christ to make the crooked ways straight. Wise guides pray that your trust is in Christ, the conductor of your life and work. Prayerfully invite these wise guides, who are passionate about prayer, to go to God on your behalf. As you debrief together on what He is doing, your intimacy with the Lord and with each other will grow, and the wisest way for you to go will be marked more clearly.

Make me know Your ways, O LORD;
Teach me Your paths.
Lead me in Your truth and teach me,
For You are the God of my salvation;
For You I wait all the day (Psalm 25:4-5 NASB).

Whom can I ask to be a wise guide in my life? Who will pray I walk in wisdom and keep on the path of Christ?

Related Readings
1 Samuel 12:23-24; Isaiah 2:3; Acts 13:9-10; Hebrews 12:11-13

11

Prarerful Perseverance

*The path of the righteous is like the morning sun,
shining ever brighter till the full light of day.*

Proverbs 4:18

Prayerful perseverance is the path of the righteous. It is the route the righteous take during recessionary times. Economic downturns can tempt us to take a detour in our walk with Christ, or they can shed light on where God wants us to go. When you persevere in prayer, the voices of worry will eventually go mute, and your Master will guide you onto a productive path.

Recessions also force us to be creative and resourceful in our relationships. Consider reaching out to those who have helped you in the past but now need your help. For example, spend time with those who are out of work, and help them find opportunities that match their calling. Most importantly, ask others how you can specifically pray for them. The Lord leads by the light of His love during dark days, so stay connected to Christ and people in prayer. This righteous resolve takes focus and hard work.

You need to persevere so that when you
have done the will of God, you will receive
what he has promised (Hebrews 10:36).

The spirit is willing, but the flesh is weak. This is why it is imperative you feed your spirit in persistent prayer. Stay engaged with God. The gleaming dawn of hope will rise on your shadowed circumstances. As you prayerfully walk with the Lord in the light, a holy security, a serene spirit shines forth from your countenance for all to see. Your humble and good works on earth bring glory to your Father in heaven.

Prayerful perseverance increases the brightness of your light like the rising of the sun. So use recessionary days to heal the hurting, rescue the repentant, and comfort the broken. Dark days are opportunities for Christians to demonstrate their faith, compassion, and generosity. Therefore, prayerfully persevere for your soul's sake, for God's glory, and in service to others.

> Then your light will break out like the dawn,
> And your recovery will speedily spring forth;
> And your righteousness will go before you;
> The glory of the LORD will be your rear guard
>   (Isaiah 58:8 NASB).

Where do I need to persevere in prayer, and whom can I specifically pray for in their dark night of the soul?

Related Readings
Job 22:28; Matthew 5:16; 26:41 KJV; Philippians 2:15

Guard Your Heart

━━━━━━━━━━━ ∞ ━━━━━━━━━━━

Above all else, guard your heart,
for everything you do flows from it.

Proverbs 4:23

G uard your heart, for it is here the Lord gives life. It is truly life because it bubbles up with tremendous trust in Him. A heart on guard for God deeply desires to love Him and obey His ways. There is a compelling call to follow Christ through the best and worst of circumstances.

Therefore, guard your heart from disbelief so doubt does not turn to despair. Guard your heart from unforgiveness so anger does not become bitterness. Guard your heart from pornography so lust does not become lasciviousness. Guard your heart from worry so fear does not become frantic. Guard your heart from pride so your attitude does not become arrogant.

A guarded heart increases the probability that you will receive good things from God. A guarded inward man makes for a good outward man.

━━━━━ ∞ ━━━━━

And the peace of God, which transcends all
understanding, will guard your hearts and
your minds in Christ Jesus (Philippians 4:7).

So how do you guard your heart from being defiled by sin and disturbed by trouble? Use wisdom in what you watch because "the eye is the lamp of the body" (Matthew 6:22). Be watchful about what words enter your ears—if you listen to lies over and over again, you are more likely to begin believing them. Ask God to be the guardian of where you go because your environment greatly influences the outcome of your heart.

A guarded heart is a candidate for greatness with God. Ask the Holy Spirit to hunker down in your heart and bring bold leadership to your life and swift conviction to your soul. Be on guard, and a wellspring of life will gush forth for God's glory.

———— ∞∞ ————

May these words of my mouth and this meditation
of my heart
be pleasing in your sight,
LORD, my Rock and my Redeemer (Psalm 19:14).

Whom can I ask to hold me accountable in what I watch so my heart is clean and pure?

Related Readings
Deuteronomy 4:9; Psalm 139:23-24; Jeremiah 17:9; Mark 7:21-23

Pay Attention

―――――⚬⚬⚬―――――

My son, pay attention to my wisdom;
turn your ear to my words of insight.

Proverbs 5:1

Pay attention to wise and discerning people around you. They have perspective that can penetrate your bias and blind spots. If you ignore their admonishments, you may miss God's best or spend a long time recovering from a raw deal. Wisdom is a watchman that keeps us from entering into unfit relationships. Beware of those who want only for you to meet their needs and have no regard for the needs of others.

Pay attention so you will not be drawn into a situation that saps your energy and leads you down an unproductive path. Cut your losses quickly. Leave the consequences in Christ's hands. For example, say no to an opportunity that does not seem right even if the promised results are positive. Pay attention to wise counsel so you will not worry later whether you did the right thing. Maintain discretion and preserve knowledge by taking time to listen and learn.

―――――⚬⚬⚬―――――

If you listen carefully to the LORD your God and do
what is right in his eyes, if you pay attention to his
commands and keep all his decrees, I will not bring
on you any of the diseases I brought on the Egyptians,
for I am the LORD, who heals you (Exodus 15:26).

Above all else, pay attention to the promptings of the Holy Spirit, who is at home in your heart and mind. He is the Almighty's ambassador in charge of leading you to the way of wisdom. Watch for His confirmation of right and His conviction of wrong. Pay attention because the Holy Spirit builds wisdom with insight and understanding. Wisdom grows in a life submitted to the guidance of God's Spirit.

Finally, pay attention to the teaching of your pastor or priest, for they are messengers of the Lord. Their role is to relay to you the truth of God, so make sure to attend church where Christ is worshipped and you are clearly and practically instructed from the Bible. Pastors who are gifted teachers and who prayerfully prepare each Sunday can present a spiritual smorgasbord so starving souls are satisfied by the wisdom of God. Pay attention to a pastor you respect, who teaches wisdom well, and whom God uses to transform your thinking and behavior.

The lips of a priest should preserve knowledge, and men should seek instruction from his mouth; for he is the messenger of the LORD of hosts (Malachi 2:7 NASB).

Who currently has my attention who should not, and whom do I need to listen to more intently with a goal to change?

Related Readings
Genesis 49:2; Mark 4:23; James 1:19; Revelation 2:7-11

Deadly Adultery

※

Her feet go down to death;
her steps lead straight to the grave.

Proverbs 5:5

Adultery is deadly. It kills relationships and destroys reputations. Children of a parent caught in adultery become confused, dismayed, and angry. A child is innocent of a parent's infidelity but still suffers the ongoing consequences of conflict, pain, and resentment. Without trust in the Lord and the transforming power of the Holy Spirit's healing and forgiveness, suffering children are set on a similar path of destruction.

Indeed, the ripple effect of adultery can be felt for generations, so run from this raw deal. It is not worth breaking the heart of God and those who love you the most. Do not allow instant gratification to numb you from the devastating effect of selfish whims. What is done in the darkness will come to light, and it is detrimental. Like the insidious work of termites, infidelity will destroy your home from the inside out as integrity's foundation begins to crumble.

※

He will bring to light what is hidden in darkness and
will expose the motives of the heart (1 Corinthians 4:5).

On the other hand, if you will remain faithful to your bride or groom, you will reap the rewards of relational life and respect from your children.

How can you be on guard against adultery's allurement? One way is to avoid websites that offer virtual temptation. We mock God when we pray, "Lead us not into temptation" (Matthew 6:13) and then expose ourselves to escapades that lead to adultery. So ask for accountability, and install software that blocks bad sites.

Also, save emotional intimacy and time alone for your spouse only. Heart connection should occur only between a husband and wife. Friendly flirtation is the first step into adultery's intoxicating control, so inoculate your life from adultery's infection with a healthy marriage. Husbands and wives who are emotionally and physically fulfilled at home are not easily led astray.

Moreover, make loving the Lord and obeying His commands your compelling commitment. God's discipline is sure for those who select the sinful action of adultery. Yes, He forgives, but He also disciplines those whom He loves. Therefore, remain on the high road of faith and fidelity. Avoid the death of adultery with a life-giving marriage.

———— ∞ ————

Marriage should be honored by all, and the marriage
bed kept pure, for God will judge the adulterer
and all the sexually immoral (Hebrews 13:4).

Who will hold me accountable, specifically regarding wisdom with my time and freedom?

Related Readings
Genesis 39:7-10; Judges 16:5-15; Matthew 5:27-30; 1 Timothy 1:9-11

Midlife Crisis

———— ∞∞ ————

May your fountain be blessed,
and may you rejoice in the wife of your youth.
A loving doe, a graceful deer—
may her breasts satisfy you always,
may you ever be intoxicated with her love.

Proverbs 5:18-19

A midlife crisis can be a sign that you are discontent. You may be discontent with your mate, your work, your car…But the Bible is clear about being content with God's blessings to you—especially your spouse. His desire is for you to want what you have and not obsess over what you do not have.

Husband, remember the bride of your youth. Perhaps you married her because she was cute and cuddly, she cared about you, and she loved Christ. Those are compelling characteristics that may have continued to grow over the years. Be joyful in Jesus and grateful to God that He has given you a woman who walks with Him and wants to be with you. Rejoice in the wife of your youth as she keeps you young and yearning for Yahweh.

———— ∞∞ ————

I am not saying this because I am in need,
for I have learned to be content whatever
the circumstances (Philippians 4:11).

Moreover, be captivated by the love of your wife. Her capacity and willingness to love you will grow as you consistently and unconditionally love her. What wife will not embrace her husband who serves her the way his Savior Jesus serves? Love and respect lead to even more love and respect. It is a Christlike cycle. Be captivated by the love of your wife, knowing she was given to you by God. You chose her, so be pleased with your choice. In His providence, He pronounced you husband and wife.

Though directed to husbands, this passage speaks to women as well. A wife captivates her husband with her kind character and attractive looks. You wooed the husband of your youth by your sweet spirit, your delightful smell, and your inviting beauty. Be intentional to make your love interesting to your husband, who may be easily bored in the bedroom. Let the distractions of life and the activities of raising children rank second to your captivating love for each other. The will of God is for you to stay faithful as husband and wife. This is the true goal for marriages that stay together.

—————∞∞∞—————

As the bridegroom rejoices over the bride,
So your God will rejoice over you (Isaiah 62:5 NASB).

How can I love my wife in a way that brings alive her captivating love?

Related Readings
Song of Songs 4:5; Ecclesiastes 9:9; 1 Corinthians 7:2; Ephesians 5:28

16

Financial Humility

⚬⚬⚬

My son, if you have put up security for your neighbor...
Go—to the point of exhaustion!—
and give your neighbor no rest!
Allow no sleep to your eyes, no slumber to your eyelids.
Free yourself.

Proverbs 6:1,3-5

It is hard to manage our own debt obligations, much less the debt commitment of another. Therefore, wisdom says to unencumber yourself from financial liability so you are free to serve. Cosigning credit on behalf of another is not smart. If you do, make plans to pay what is due. Or in bold humility, go to the one for whom you partnered or cosigned, and ask if you can get out from under the financial obligation.

Even if you pay a penalty for backing out, what price would you pay for your newfound peace of mind? Financial overextension is unwise. Consider consolidating your credit and making a bold plan to pay down your personal debt. Debt reduction is smart, especially during recessionary times. "The borrower is slave to the lender" (Proverbs 22:7), so in humility and boldness you can break the chain of financial servitude.

⚬⚬⚬

You were bought at a price; do not become slaves
of human beings (1 Corinthians 7:23 NASB).

Limiting credit or abolishing it completely is countercultural. But why make credit convenient to a spender who struggles to stay within a budget? Therefore, apply discipline and sacrifice. You can experience the peaceful result of debt-free living.

There is one other word related to cosigning. You may know a young person who needs someone to vouch for his or her character and credit. The apostle Paul guaranteed the servant Onesimus's repayment, and you may be led to do the same for someone. Perhaps you ultimately see your assistance as a gift—if you are paid back, it is an unexpected bonus. Relationships are much more valuable than cash. Regardless of the stressful situation, make sure you manage expectations with prayerful prudence and bold humility.

If then you consider me a partner and a comrade in fellowship, welcome and receive him as you would [welcome and receive] me. And if he has done you any wrong in any way or owes anything [to you], charge that to my account. I, Paul, write it with my own hand, I promise to repay it [in full] (Philemon 1:17-19 AMP).

Whom do I need to boldly but humbly approach about dissolving a financial arrangement?

Related Readings
Deuteronomy 8:17-18; Romans 13:8; James 2:6

Plan Ahead

Go to the ant, you sluggard;
consider its ways and be wise!
It has no commander, no overseer or ruler,
yet it stores its provisions in summer
and gathers its food at harvest.

Proverbs 6:6-8

Wisdom works hard now and is wise about planning for the future. Planners have an innate sense of discipline. Imminently urgent matters do not distract them as they stay focused on important issues. Their discipline determines the choices they make during the day because they are always keenly aware that their actions affect their future. The best planners take the time to process assumptions and the implications of best-case and worst-case scenarios.

Self-motivated and disciplined planners do not require rigid management and control. They thrive in autonomy even while submitting to the accountability of authority. Wise planners save time and money. Their decision-making filter says no more often than yes—even to good opportunities. The Holy Spirit works through a prayerfully crafted plan to guide you into God's best, so stay aligned with the plan.

Many are the plans in a person's heart,
but it is the LORD's purpose that
prevails (Proverbs 19:21).

Ants are tiny, but their unified effort brings large results. A clearly defined, well-executed plan brings your team together and produces an outstanding outcome. A plan creates credibility and gives courage to those who implement it. So be sensitive to your season of strategic service.

If you are in the preparation phase, be patient and focused on the plan. If you are in the execution phase, remain diligent and focused on the task at hand. As you harvest success, make sure to save for the future. Abundance is not meant to be spent all at once but to be saved for the downtimes. Use your church, business, or home as a platform of provision for others in need. Plan ahead so you can be an ambassador for Almighty God.

———— ∞ ————

Instruct them to do good, to be rich in good works,
to be generous and ready to share, storing up
for themselves the treasure of a good foundation
for the future, so that they may take hold of that
which is life indeed (1 Timothy 6:18-19 NASB).

What opportunities do I need to put on hold so I can focus on implementing the current strategic plan with excellence?

Related Readings
Genesis 41:28-43; Job 12:7-8; Luke 14:28; Hebrews 6:11-12

Lustful Longings

〜

*Do not lust in your heart after her beauty
or let her captivate you with her eyes.*

Proverbs 6:25

Lustful longings lead us away from loving the Lord because our affections become attached to something that is not ours. What seems like innocent flattery quickly grows into emotional attachment. Our emotions are meant for intimacy with our spouse and none other. Confiding in a beautiful person other than your spouse may feel good, but it is a problem waiting to happen.

If your coworker or friend makes your heart race and is the subject of racy fantasies, you need to flee. You may need to transfer your assistant to another department or even let him or her go. You are flirting with fire when you forge ahead in relationships that enflame your lust, so douse the flames by walking away and setting up accountability systems.

〜

> Can you build a fire in your lap
>   and not burn your pants?
> Can you walk barefoot on hot coals
>   and not get blisters?
> It's the same when you have sex with your
>   neighbor's wife:
>   Touch her and you'll pay for it.
>   No excuses (Proverbs 6:27-28 MSG).

The Internet can become a contributor to lustful longings, a tool for good that Satan uses for evil. Make sure others monitor your machine so your heart and mind do not meander to illicit images. Install computer software that forces you to be selective in your web surfing, producing a report to be reviewed by an accountability partner.

Moreover, make it your motivation and desire to pursue loving God and loving people. This will crowd out fleshly lusts from your heart. The Bible says, "Flee from youthful lusts and pursue righteousness, faith, love and peace, with those who call on the Lord with a pure heart" (2 Timothy 2:22 NASB). You can do your soul a great kindness by distancing yourself from sin and detesting the sight of it. Eyes focused on fidelity, faith, and authentic love lead to freedom empowered by the Holy Spirit.

Walk by the Spirit, and you will not carry out
the desire of the flesh (Galatians 5:16).

How can I protect my eyes from lustful images, focusing instead on the beauty of my spouse?

Related Readings
Genesis 39:8-10; Job 31:1-12; Matthew 5:28; 1 Peter 2:11

19

Leaders Learn

———— ⊂∞⊃ ————

Say to wisdom, "You are my sister,"
and to insight, "You are my relative."

Proverbs 7:4

Leaders are learners. When they stop learning, they cease to lead wisely. Education is a hallmark of leaders who think ahead and are engaged in effective execution. If a leader does not assess the facts of a situation and operate in reality, he loses any advantage he might possess. Circumspect living characterizes leaders who are ever learning.

A leader continually asks questions like these: "How can we better understand what the customer wants and needs?" "How can I get out of the way as the leader, helping the team to succeed?" "How can our organization go from good to great by integrating and sustaining the industry's best practices?" Leaders who learn to ask the right questions get the most accurate answers and are able to make the wisest decisions.

———— ⊂∞⊃ ————

Jehoshaphat also said to the king of Israel, "First seek the counsel of the Lord" (1 Kings 22:5).

Leaders learn by listening to the Lord and to the wisdom found in His Word. Learning is not a one-time event but the ongoing purging of pride, pretense, and prayerlessness. Wisdom becomes a beloved sister to whom you go for counsel. Humility grows into a trusted friend with whom you can confide.

The Holy Bible is your defense and armor against the assault of unwise thinking. Therefore, read and study the Word of God and apply it regularly to your life. Read books that highlight examples of other leaders worth emulating. Learn by listening to teachers who communicate truth with clarity and conviction. Learn from your mistakes, and do not repeat them. Learn forgiveness from your family, service from your friends, and love from your enemies.

If you have any encouragement from being
united with Christ, if any comfort from his love, if
any fellowship with the Spirit, if any tenderness
and compassion, then make my joy complete by
being like-minded, having the same love, being
one in spirit and of one mind (Philippians 2:1-2).

What life lessons do I need to currently learn so the Lord can entrust me with further educational opportunities?

Related Readings
Deuteronomy 6:6-9; Psalm 90:12; 2 Corinthians 3:3; 2 Timothy 4:13

False Spirituality

*She took hold of him and kissed him
and with a brazen face she said:
"Today I fulfilled my vows,
and I have food from my fellowship offering at home."*

Proverbs 7:13-14

Unfortunately, some folks use religion to get their way. They may be single adults who prey on unsuspecting singles in church. They attend church to take advantage of trusting souls. Some businessmen use the art of Christian conversation to give the appearance of values and principles based on the Bible. However, once they make the sale or close the deal, their self-serving and dishonest ways reveal who they really are.

Spiritual deception—using God to get our way—is one of the worst types of deceit. A husband may use submission to control his wife, or a wife may use grace to withhold herself from her husband. Others, like Simon in the early church, may even try to buy the Holy Spirit for their benefit. Cultivate authentic spirituality in your heart and mind through prayer, worship, and community.

Such regulations indeed have an appearance
of wisdom, with their self-imposed worship,
their false humility and their harsh treatment of
the body, but they lack any value in restraining
sensual indulgence (Colossians 2:23).

True spirituality, on the other hand, is motivated and controlled by the Spirit of Christ. It is authentic because Almighty God is the initiator. True spirituality is not just looking out for itself but is sincerely concerned with serving others. You are comfortable with people who are developing true spirituality because you know they care for you. Integrity characterizes their business and religious activities. Their yes is yes, and their no is no. There are no surprises—what you see is what you get.

True spirituality grows over time. It is forged on the anvil of adversity, taught at the hearth of humility, and received at the gate of God's grace. You know your religion is real when you prioritize love for others above your own needs and you care for the poor and needy. True spirituality inspires others to love God and obey His commands.

Pure and undefiled religion in the sight of our
God and Father is this: to visit orphans and
widows in their distress, and to keep oneself
unstained by the world (James 1:27 NASB).

How have I been tempted to appear spiritual while asserting my own will?

Related Readings
Ecclesiastes 7:4; Matthew 25:36; Acts 8:19-20; 2 Corinthians 1:17

21

Travel Temptations

———— ∞ ————

My husband is not at home;
he has gone on a long journey.
He took his purse filled with money
and will not be home till full moon.

Proverbs 7:19-20

How do you deal with temptations when you travel? What is your behavior when you are the spouse left at home? Is your house a palace of peace or a prison of confinement? Whether you are the weary traveler or the one left holding down the fort, be wary of wrong behavior. As a couple, consider crafting guidelines of what you will and will not do when you are apart.

Distance can make the heart grow fonder and more faithful, but it can also fan the flames of lust and infidelity. If you travel for your work, you most likely are motivated to meet the needs of your family. However, every assignment is for a season. Maybe it's time to get off the road and reconnect with your child who is approaching the teen years. Perhaps you need to be there more often for your spouse, who is starved for extra emotional support. Be willing to adjust.

———— ∞ ————

Do not be misled: "Bad company corrupts
good character." Come back to your senses
as you ought, and stop sinning; for there are
some who are ignorant of God—I say this
to your shame (1 Corinthians 15:33-34).

Be careful not to drift into travel temptations that become divisive and deteriorate your marriage. One boundary may be to avoid bars and get back to your room soon after work and dinner. A righteous routine on the road gets the right results. Whenever possible, travel with another person of the same gender who shares your values. Be bold by becoming an influencer of integrity. Enjoy good, clean fun without flirting with sin.

On the other hand, your role in the marriage may be to support the children and manage the home daily. Take pride during this season of unselfish service. Resist the temptation to look for pity. By God's grace you are conforming your children's minds to the things of Christ, influencing the culture with His kingdom priorities. As you are working to preserve the family, you are as valuable as the one who is away, working to provide for the family. Stay occupied in prayer, Bible study, and your kids' school, and be available to those who need you.

Marriage is a team effort. You'll see outstanding results when you are on the same page of love and obedience to Christ. Travel temptations are terminated on both ends through trust in the Lord and trust in each other.

———— ✷ ————

> "He trusts in the LORD," they say,
>   "let the LORD rescue him.
> Let him deliver him,
>   since he delights in him" (Psalm 22:8).

What travel boundaries do my spouse and I need to create?

Related Readings
Numbers 5:11-15; Isaiah 46:6; Luke 12:39-46; 1 John 3:9

22

Hate Evil

To fear the Lord is to hate evil;
I hate pride and arrogance,
evil behavior and perverse speech.

Proverbs 8:13

The word "hate" makes us uncomfortable. It has a harsh and uncaring ring and reputation. However, Almighty God allows and even expects a holy hatred of evil. Authentic Christianity is not easy on evil, which breaks God's heart and destroys people's souls. Evil is the enemy's encroachment on eternity's agenda.

Evil takes down leaders who let pride and arrogance seep into their minds and stay there. Indeed, if the rules apply to everyone but the leader, then it is just a matter of time before the humble fear of the Lord gives way to prideful indulgence. Sin is out of bounds for any child of God who abides in the love and grace of God. The wisdom of Christ warms the heart, instructs the mind, and leads the way into behavior defined by truth.

The full assurance of understanding [results] in a true knowledge of God's mystery, that is, Christ Himself, in whom are hidden all the treasures of wisdom and knowledge (Colossians 2:2-3 NASB).

Gossip, greed, jealousy, and lies are all evil intentions that corrupt a culture of transparency, generosity, contentment, and honesty. Stress can bring out the best and worst in others, so by the grace of God, make sure you rise above the petty politics of blame. Let your wisdom and maturity be on display as you lead others (your children, friends, coworkers…) by choosing to live according to a higher standard. If you do nothing, the naysayers will cause fear and division.

Fight evil without fanfare. By faith and wise work, deliver constant, creditable results, and your antagonists will grow quiet. The humility and wisdom of Christ will defeat evil initiatives. Therefore, give Him the glory, get the job done, and trust the Lord with the results. Hard times can produce hard hearts unless you overcome evil with a humble heart of prayer and bold faith. Evil is extinguished with the fervent prayers of people who are committed to purity.

Make this your common practice: Confess your sins
to each other and pray for each other so that you
can live together whole and healed. The prayer
of a person living right with God is something
powerful to be reckoned with (James 5:16-17 MSG).

What does a holy hatred of evil look like in my life?

Related Readings
Amos 5:15; Zechariah 8:17; Romans 12:9; 2 Timothy 2:19

Political Wisdom

————— ०∞० —————

*By [wisdom] kings reign
and rulers make laws that are just;
by [wisdom] princes govern,
and nobles—all who rule on earth.*

Proverbs 8:15-16

The wisdom of God overshadows the best and brightest thinking of man. This is why our American ancestors looked to the Almighty for knowledge and understanding when crafting our constitution. Its remarkable effectiveness is contingent on faith in God, faith in government, and faith in the citizens. Indeed, politicians who plead with Providence for wisdom will become the wiser. Rulers who recognize their authority is from God will rule for God.

A humble ambition accompanies the most effective statesmen into public service. They exchange their political pride for humble wisdom. Leaders rule others wisely when religion rules their own conscience and character. Political wisdom is a prerequisite for public servants who would govern in alignment with the principles of Providence on behalf of the people. These wise rulers are able to rest in peace in the middle of a storm.

————— ०∞० —————

For the one in authority is God's servant for
your good. But if you do wrong, be afraid, for
rulers do not bear the sword for no reason.

> They are God's servants, agents of wrath to bring
> punishment on the wrongdoer (Romans 13:4).

A culture thrown into economic chaos especially needs principled men and women to step up, sacrifice, and make hard decisions. In the middle of extreme uncertainty, wise leaders must sometimes make painful prescriptions to prevent further panic. They must determine what is best for the whole in the long term, and the stakes are high. Pray for political leaders to look beyond themselves and to see past short-term relief into the perspective and principles of God found in holy Scripture.

Indeed, wise political leaders pray for intervention and understanding from the Almighty. Perhaps during desperate days, a filibuster of faith is first needed, so these leaders start by looking and listening to the Lord. Just laws follow political wisdom, which does what Christ defines as right. Wise politicians keep their hands of faithfulness on the Bible's principles and their hearts submitted to the Lord's authority. Presidents honor Him by never forgetting their sacred inaugural vow, "So help me God."

―∞∞―

> Blessed be the LORD your God who delighted in you
> to set you on the throne of Israel; because the LORD
> loved Israel forever, therefore He made you king, to
> do justice and righteousness (1 Kings 10:9 NASB).

How can I promote political wisdom with the public servants in my circle of influence?

Related Readings
Psalm 148:11-13; Daniel 2:21-47; Romans 13:1; Revelation 19:11-16

God's Favor

∞

Blessed are those who listen to me [wisdom],
watching daily at my doors, waiting at my doorway.
For whoever finds me finds life and
receives favor from the LORD.

Proverbs 8:34-35

G od's favor rests on those who find wisdom. They seek wisdom by first watching at the doors of heaven, waiting patiently at the feet of their Savior Jesus. It is humbling to think that each day Almighty God is available to renew our commission to serve the cause of Christ. We pursue Jesus's wisdom because His is pure and profound.

As in the days of Cain and Abel, the Almighty continues to bless the best offering. Therefore, honor God by offering Him the firstfruits of your day. Just as He deserves first dibs on your money, so He expects the beginning of your day. Get up and go to God first. There you discover a wealth of wisdom, and as you rest in the shadow of your Savior Jesus Christ, you receive His favor.

∞

Then that person can pray to God and find favor
  with him,
    they will see God's face and shout for joy;
    he will restore them to full well-being (Job 33:26).

Happiness comes to those who wait for wisdom. God's blessing cannot be rushed, so rest in Him. God's favor is well worth the wait.

Like a newborn when it arrives, God's favor brings joy that is unspeakable. How many times have we rushed ahead, outside the canopy of Christ's blessing? The Israelites learned to stay under the cloud of God and be led by faith. Indeed, those who step outside God's favor suffer for lack of spiritual oxygen. However, those who enjoy their heavenly Father's favor also enjoy deep rest.

His blessing provides strength for the journey, empowering you to persevere as you follow the trail of trust. Jesus experienced the favor of His heavenly Father when He submitted to public baptism, which was His confession of faith, His commitment to public service, and His commission to ministry. What issue of obedience are you facing today? What wise choices can you make that will enable you to continually experience the favor of your heavenly Father? Your life is alive and vibrant because the Lord favors you. You are a favorite of your heavenly Father because you are learning to wait on Him and humbly walk with the wise.

He has told you, O man, what is good;
And what does the LORD require of you
But to do justice, to love kindness,
And to walk humbly with your God?
(Micah 6:8 NASB).

How can I continually position myself to receive God's favor and blessing?

Related Readings
Genesis 4:4; Exodus 33:12; Luke 2:52; Philippians 3:8

25

Choose Your Battles

———— ✾ ————

Whoever corrects a mocker invites insults;
whoever rebukes the wicked incurs abuse.

Proverbs 9:7

We all have a limited amount of time and energy. Wisdom says to spend them both on productive people, not destructive ones. Verbal sparring with those who are proud only invites insult. It is better to ignore their rants than try to reason with them. Do your best, stay focused on the task, and trust your reputation with the giver of reputations—your Savior Jesus.

Mockers look to stir up things in the moment. They have no long-term solutions, so avoid their cynical, crazy-making cycle. A mocker's mind is already made up—he will not change regardless of wise rationale. There are those who return evil for good, so do not go there, or you may end up in despair. Jesus says the caustic cynic is full of pride.

———— ✾ ————

Let them alone; they are blind guides of the
blind. And if a blind man guides a blind man,
both will fall into a pit (Matthew 15:14 NASB).

What about a family member who seems to be hurtling down a path of destruction? What if teenagers or adult children set their entire focus on friends and freedom and seem to have rejected all common sense and Christlike influences? First, focus on their heart with love and acceptance. If you spar over externals, the battle will be messy and costly. However, if they change from the inside out, the transformation will be beautiful and enduring.

Invite them to pray, asking the Lord what He thinks about their decisions and choice of friends. Direct them back to Scripture as their Savior's standard for living. Above all, pursue a peaceful and patient attitude in prayer. Our most significant battles are spiritual—they are won or lost on our knees. The Holy Spirit will lead you when to speak, what to say, and when to remain silent. Everyone wins when you value the relationship more than winning the argument.

Do not rebuke mockers or they will hate you;
   rebuke the wise and they will love you (Proverbs 9:8).

What relationship do I need to quit striving over and give to the Lord?

Related Readings
2 Chronicles 30:7-9; Proverbs 23:9; Matthew 7:6; 22:4-6

Invite Instruction

⌒⌒⌒

Rebuke the wise and they will love you.
Instruct the wise and they will be wiser still;
teach the righteous and they will add to their learning.

Proverbs 9:8-9

Wise people invite instruction. They understand that correction and rebuke are necessary if they are to grow in wisdom and righteous behavior. Without well-meaning instructors willing to get in our faces, we aspire to be average at best. However, an invitation to meddle in our affairs sets the stage for authentic accountability. Effective correction makes us uncomfortable at times, but we become wiser as a result. Indeed, conflict is inherent in accountability.

So if your relationships are conflict free, perhaps no one is holding you accountable in a significant way. Wisdom comes to us in raw relationships that can stand the strain of loving reproof and are characterized by a willingness to change. A rebuke wakes you up and alerts you to the realities you are facing. Your spouse is not nagging, but nudging you to act responsibly. Therefore, invite instruction, and you will increase in wisdom and understanding. Wise recipients of reproof have no regrets.

⌒⌒⌒

Like an earring of gold or an ornament of fine gold
is the rebuke of a wise judge to a listening ear
(Proverbs 25:12).

Also, be willing to be the bearer of bad news. With love and grace, go to your friend who has asked for your counsel, and give him or her truth. Pray first and then deliver the unpleasant news. It is much better for others to see the error of their ways now than to reach a point of no return. Talk to them, not about them. Pray for them privately, not publically with a pious prayer request.

Love motivates rebuke and then becomes a recipient of love. Your relationship will dissolve in anger or rise to a higher level of respect through righteous rebuke. Take the time to prod another toward perfection because you care. Be respectful and instruct with patience. One day the student's wisdom may exceed that of the teacher.

The student is not above the teacher, but everyone
who is fully trained will be like their teacher (Luke 6:40).

To whom do I need to listen, learning from their correction and rebuke?

Related Readings
Psalm 141:5; 2 Peter 3:18; 2 Timothy 4:2; Revelation 3:19

27

The Beginning of Wisdom

The fear of the LORD is the beginning of wisdom,
and knowledge of the Holy One is understanding.

Proverbs 9:10

The fear of the Lord is fundamental to finding wisdom. Without awe of the Almighty, there is no access to His insights. Reverence for God's holiness is a requisite for understanding His ways. The first step in acquiring wisdom from Almighty God is to fear Him—to worship His majesty and dread His judgment.

God's holy Word—the Bible—is to be taken to heart as truth for the purpose of life transformation. At first, the fear of the Lord may be so overwhelming that we struggle to sense His love, and our desire for intimacy goes unmet. Anyone who has been broken understands this process. However, once we embrace a healthy fear of the Lord, the result is peace and knowledge in submission to and love for the Holy One.

He will be the sure foundation for your times,
    a rich store of salvation and wisdom and knowledge;
the fear of the LORD is the key to this treasure
    (Isaiah 33:6).

We mock God when we move away from the language of fear, and He is not one to be mocked. So as devoted followers of Christ, let's sow the seeds of respect, reverence, and the fear of the Lord. This discipline of faith results in a harvest of holiness, happiness, and wisdom. Fear of Him leads to knowledge of Him. Therefore, bowing before Him on your knees in prayer, seek His face for forgiveness and relational restoration.

Celebrate together with Christ our conquest over sin, sorrow, and death. What is counterintuitive on earth is intuitive in heaven. Listen to David admonish his son Solomon, who became the wisest man in the world:

> As for you, my son Solomon, know the God of your father, and serve Him with a whole heart and a willing mind; for the LORD searches all hearts, and understands every intent of the thoughts. If you seek Him, He will let you find Him; but if you forsake Him, He will reject you forever (1 Chronicles 28:9 NASB).

What area of my life lacks the fear of the Lord, and how can I make myself more accountable?

Related Readings
Job 28:28; Psalm 111:10; Matthew 11:27; 1 John 5:20

Love Forgives

Hatred stirs up dissension,
but love covers over all wrongs.

Proverbs 10:12

True love forgives regardless of the infraction because it transcends mistreatment.

What is your standard for forgiveness? Is it conditional, based on the way you are treated, or is it unconditional? Hatred has no hope but to stir up dissension and rally a defense. However, love looks at being wronged as an opportunity to replace insult with encouragement. Love seeks to lead all parties into a better place of health and happiness.

Indeed, hatred finds no home in a heart of love. It sows discord, but love plants peace. It embraces enmity, while love exudes compassion. Hate stirs up, but love calms down. How do you handle those who are hard to be around? Perhaps out of love you serve them. Seek to serve rather than be served.

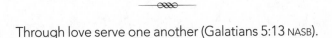

Through love serve one another (Galatians 5:13 NASB).

Love forgives because you have been forgiven by the matchless love of God. The Lord's love toward you empowers you to lovingly forgive another. Apart from God, human love is unable to love without boundaries. Left to our own limited love, we love only those who love us. Jesus said, "If you love only those who love you, what reward is there for that? Even corrupt tax collectors do that much" (Matthew 5:46 NLT).

Therefore, look at love as an opportunity to give others what they do not deserve. Lean on the Lord as your source of unconditional love. Christ's love is all-inclusive and all-forgiving. In the same way, actively and appropriately love those in your life—maybe with a kind word, a nice note of appreciation, a thoughtful gift, or a listening ear. Harness your love into a habit of forgiveness.

———∞∞∞———

Most important of all, continue to show
deep love for each other, for love covers
a multitude of sins (1 Peter 4:8 NLT).

Whom do I need to love, forgive, and serve in honor of God's great love?

Related Readings
Leviticus 19:17; Proverbs 17:9; Philippians 1:9; 1 John 4:20-21

29

Tempered Talk

⸺⸺⸺ ∞∞ ⸺⸺⸺

Sin is not ended by multiplying words,
but the prudent hold their tongues.

Proverbs 10:19

Tempered talk is a sign of wise conversation. When our words are many, we run the risk of soliciting sin. Increased words increase the probability of improper speech. For example, respectful conversation does not repeat the same words and phrases in a short time. This impatient cadence frustrates.

Perhaps a look of misunderstanding requires questions for clarification or definitions for comprehension. Proud conversationalists can highjack a listener's understanding with a horde of words without meaning. If your goal is to communicate, take the time to listen to the needs of your audience. People who feel cared for and understood have a keener sense of hearing and understanding.

⸺⸺ ∞∞ ⸺⸺

Even fools are thought wise if they keep silent,
and discerning if they hold their tongues
(Proverbs 17:28).

Wise people weigh their words before they speak. They allow their minds to catch up with their hearts. Furthermore, in the face of wrong behavior, emotions sometimes need to be expressed If you feel mistreated or misinformed, let the other person know. Concealed anger leads to living a lie (see Proverbs 10:18), but tempered talk is truthful and to the point.

Reserve your words out of respect for the other person. If you do all the talking, you are the center of attention. We are being condescending when the people we are conversing with don't feel important enough to speak up. So honor others by speaking less and listening more intently to learn how you can love them. Wisdom can be found in the words of each person you meet. Therefore, intentionally talk less and be wise.

—oᴚᴂᴑ—

My dear brothers, take note of this: Everyone
should be quick to listen, slow to speak and
slow to become angry (James 1:19).

Whom do I need to listen to more? When am I usually tempted to talk too much?

Related Readings
Job 2:3; Amos 5:13; Titus 1:10; James 3:2

30

Economic Storms

*When the storm has swept by, the wicked are gone,
but the righteous stand firm forever.*

Proverbs 10:25

When the ocean tide goes out, rocks and waterlogged driftwood that are normally hidden under the water become visible. In the same way, economic storms expose hidden evil.

The wicked may seem to be prospering, but eventually they will be found out. The Holy Spirit shakes out sin so it can be seen and judged. As the Lord promised His children in the past, "I will shake the people of Israel" (Amos 9:9).

Why make a lot of noise, draw people's attention, and then lose your creditability under scrutiny? During economic storms, businesses and ministries that depend on debt collapse, and solid churches increase in attendance. There is a purging of pride, and all manner of excess is exposed. The things that really matter in life receive our attention—faith, family, friends, food, and shelter. Storms reveal worth.

Those who cling to Christ are not shaken. He is our cornerstone, which no degree of chaos can challenge. The righteous cannot be moved because their Master is immovable. Therefore, stand firm in the Lord.

Those who trust in the LORD are like Mount Zion,
which cannot be shaken but endures forever
(Psalm 125:1).

Worldly wisdom has a way of reducing heaven's wisdom to an afterthought. Sometimes we pray, seeking to discern the Lord's way, but only after we've tried our own way—to no avail. We are often tempted to rely on what seems to work instead of asking what principles to live by based on God's economy.

Your stability in your Savior provides security for your family, friends, and coworkers. Your unwavering faith during difficult days helps them replace panic with peace, fear with faith, and compromise with conviction. If all you have left is a firm foundation of faith, begin rebuilding God's big vision. Are you a wise builder?

———

Therefore everyone who hears these words of
mine and puts them into practice is like a wise man
who built his house on the rock (Matthew 7:24).

How can I build my life, home, and work on the solid rock of Jesus?

Related Readings
Job 20:5; Psalm 37:10; Acts 2:25; Hebrews 12:28

31

A Faithful Guide

∞∞

The integrity of the upright guides them,
but the unfaithful are destroyed by their duplicity.

Proverbs 11:3

Integrity is an instrument of Almighty God. He uses it to guide His children in the direction He desires for them. Have you ever wondered what God would have you do? Integrity is His directive to do the next right thing, trusting Him with the results. Our honesty helps us to comprehend Christ's desires. He delights in our uprightness.

For example, are you totally honest on your tax return? Is your tax preparer a person of unquestionable integrity? We can trust professionals to represent us well, but we are ultimately responsible for an honest outcome. Are you doing anything that would embarrass you and your family if it was printed as a newspaper headline? Integrity brings joy to heaven and security on earth. It is your guide for godly living.

∞∞

I put in charge of Jerusalem my brother Hanani,
along with Hananiah the commander of the citadel,
because he was a man of integrity and feared God
more than most people do (Nehemiah 7:2).

The iniquity of the unfaithful destroys. The blessing of God is removed because it cannot be bought with bad behavior. Relationships are scarred and some severed as a result of dishonest dealings. Overnight, poor judgment can soil and potentially destroy a hard-earned reputation. Prideful people act as if integrity is only for others. They deceive themselves and are eventually disgraced by their dishonest and duplicitous ways. On the other hand, iniquity is an unfaithful guide.

So we ask ourselves, "How can I be a man or woman of integrity over the balance of my life?" There is a simplicity about those who base their behavior on the principles in God's Word—nothing fancy, only faithful living in their daily routine. The grace of God governs their soul, the truth of God renews their mind, and accountability is an anchor for their actions. Honestly ask yourself, "Is integrity my faithful guide?"

<hr />

> May integrity and uprightness protect me,
> because my hope, LORD, is in you (Psalm 25:21).

How can I better integrate integrity as a guide for my business dealings and behavior at home?

Related Readings
Genesis 20:4-7; Hosea 13:9; Matthew 7:13; Romans 7:9-12

32

Influencing Our Cities for Christ

When the righteous prosper, the city rejoices;
when the wicked perish, there are shouts of joy.
Through the blessing of the upright a city is exalted.

Proverbs 11:10-11

How can we capture our cities for Christ? How can we help our municipalities become institutions of integrity? Perhaps it starts with each of us who claims Jesus Christ as Savior. It's up to us to first get down on our knees and get down to business with our heavenly Father. The people of God make up the city of God. Through our own confession and repentance of sin, the city is set up to receive blessing from the Lord.

Citizens are not to be passive in the face of wickedness. Daniel understood this and prayed this passionate prayer for his city:

> Lord, in keeping with all your righteous acts, turn away your anger and your wrath from Jerusalem, your city, your holy hill. Our sins and the iniquities of our ancestors have made Jerusalem and your people an object of scorn to all those around us (Daniel 9:16).

Christ influences cities through His church when His children confess, "He is Christ, Son of the living God." When we confess Christ with our words and our life, we partner with the Holy Spirit in building the Lord's living temple—His church. His dwelling does not consist of church buildings. His dwelling is in the hearts of men, women, boys, and girls who, empowered by His grace, give others the opportunity to hear the old, old story of Jesus's love for them. Jesus is building His church for the glory of God.

A city movement for Christ is birthed out of passionate prayer and brokenness. Jesus cried out for His city. "As he approached Jerusalem and saw the city, he wept over it" (Luke 19:41). Our tears become tools the Holy Spirit can use to transform us and others. We experience healing as sorrow turns to joy. The early church rejoiced over this unleashing of the Lord's power: "So there was great joy in that city" (Acts 8:8).

A city moved along by the Holy Spirit becomes a shining light of its Savior Jesus. He exalts the community on His hill of hope so all might see, believe, and be saved. Jesus says, "You are the light of the world. A town built on a hill cannot be hidden" (Matthew 5:14). So we solemnly ask, "Have I claimed my city for Christ? Am I part of His movement?"

Whom can I invite to passionately pray with me over our city's movement toward God?

Related Readings
Genesis 41:38-42; Isaiah 16:5; Acts 13:44; 16:13-15

33

Refreshers Are Refreshed

—— ∞∞ ——

A generous man will prosper;
he who refreshes others will himself be refreshed.

Proverbs 11:25

What does it mean to be refreshed? It is to be revived, enlivened, invigorated, rejuvenated, energized, restored, recharged, or revitalized. A meager cup of lukewarm coffee comes alive with taste and satisfaction when mixed with freshly brewed beans. A lukewarm life is warmed and encouraged when refreshed with words of encouragement and acts of kindness. Everyone we meet can be a candidate for refreshment.

Our faith cools down when Christ seems silent and circumstances continue to crumble, but a sincere prayer from a righteous friend restores and warms our confidence. Our hope feels deferred in the face of disappointment and rejection, but we are energized by the acceptance and love of a community of believers in Jesus. Hope loves company. Seek refreshment from your Savior and His followers. Be refreshed so you can refresh others.

—— ∞∞ ——

I will refresh the weary and satisfy
the faint (Jeremiah 31:25).

When your parched soul has been watered by dew from heaven, you can lead others to the Lord's watering hole. People feel robbed by insensitive institutions and greedy governments, but we can reconnect them to their generous God. Jesus gives us an abundant life to share with others who lack abundance. "I have come that they may have life, and that they may have it more abundantly" (John 10:10 NKJV).

Your refreshment reciprocates refreshment. When you refresh another financially, you are refreshed by faith and fulfillment. When you refresh another emotionally, you are refreshed by peace and contentment. When you refresh another spiritually, you are refreshed by the grace and love of God. Are you in need of refreshment? If so, receive Christ's full cup of joy. Drink often with the Lord so you can generously refresh friends.

—⚉—

Taste and see that the LORD is good;
blessed is the man who takes refuge in him
(Psalm 34:8).

How can I keep refreshed so I in turn can refresh others?

Related Readings
Ruth 2:14; Psalm 41:1; Matthew 25:34-35; 2 Corinthians 9:6-7

34

A Noble Wife

A wife of noble character is her husband's crown,
but a disgraceful wife is like decay in his bones.

Proverbs 12:4

Why are certain wives attractive and others unattractive? Why do you enjoy the company of some but avoid the company of others? A wife of noble character is attractive because she aspires to obey Almighty God. She is a joy to be around because she enjoys being in the presence of the Lord. Her first allegiance is to her Savior Jesus Christ, exhibited by her regal appearance and respectful responses. God has first place in her heart.

Her husband takes pride in her because she can be trusted in all household matters and financial management. By faith she follows her husband's leadership. She entrusts him to God, to whom he is accountable. A wife of noble character knows how to prayerfully ask challenging questions of her husband without usurping his leadership. She is strong and gracious, bold and beautiful, firm and friendly, faithful and loving.

And now, my daughter, don't be afraid. I will do for
you all you ask. All the people of my town know that
you are a woman of noble character (Ruth 3:11).

She loves her children when they are unlovely and disciplines them when they behave badly. They know their mom cares even when she gets carried away in her correction. A wife of noble character is a model of motherhood for her daughters and an example of the kind of woman her sons should marry. She wisely honors her husband in front of the children, especially when she and her husband disagree. Her character is a compass for the actions of her kids.

A wife of noble character is not afraid to mentor and encourage other wives—not with a superior spirit, but with an attitude of meekness and brokenness. She quickly admits to her past mistakes, thereby saving some young women from repeating her own hurt and heartache. She remains a student even while she endeavors to teach and train. She conveys wisdom with her humble and gracious words.

A noble wife is a blessing to her husband. "She is worth far more than rubies" (Proverbs 31:10).

How can I enjoy my husband and children even more and always see them as blessings from God?

Related Readings
Genesis 2:18-24; 1 Corinthians 11:7-11; 1 Timothy 5:1-2

35

Unpretentious Living

———— ∞ ————

*Better to be a nobody and yet have a servant
than pretend to be somebody and have no food.*

Proverbs 12:9

Unpretentious living opens the door to down-to-earth interactions with others. Rest and relaxation attend to those who are true to themselves without acting like someone they are not. However, people who depend on pretentious speech and behavior have to exert extra energy to keep up the act. For them, contentment is illusive and intimacy is an illusion. I become the most stressful when I feel as if I have to live up to something or be someone I am not.

When you are real, not fake, your friends feel the freedom to be the same. You energize others rather than draining energy out of them. I have to be honest and ask often, "Am I being myself, or is the way I dress, the way I talk, what I drive, or where I live motivated by a need to be somebody I am not?" Pretense is a result of pride, but humility is the fruit of unpretentious living. Humility comes from Christ as He lives His life in and through you.

———— ∞ ————

Christ in you, the hope of glory (Colossians 1:27).

Jesus is clear: "Everyone who exalts himself will be humbled, and he who humbles himself will be exalted" (Luke 14:11 NASB). In Christ you are somebody. High or low net worth, small or large home, new or used car, prestigious university or common college, in Him you are somebody. You are somebody to your Savior Jesus.

Your simple faith and modesty make room for the Lord to take center stage in your life. Humility positions you to point people to heaven. Therefore, keep your life unencumbered so people can see your Savior shine. Ask yourself, "Whom am I trying to impress, people I really do not know or the Lover of my soul, Jesus?"

Those who want to impress people by means of the flesh are trying to compel you to be circumcised. The only reason they do this is to avoid being persecuted for the cross of Christ (Galatians 6:12).

How can I be more authentic and open with my spouse, children, and coworkers?

Related Readings

1 Samuel 16:7; Proverbs 13:7; Romans 2:28; 1 Peter 3:3-4

36

Routine Work

—∞∞—

Those who work the land will have abundant food,
but those who chase fantasies have no sense.

Proverbs 12:11

Routine work may not be sexy, but it is necessary if we are to meet our own needs and the needs of those who depend on us. The same work, day in and day out, can seem simple and boring, but it is a test of our faithfulness. Will I continue to faithfully carry out uncomplicated responsibilities, even when my attention span is suffering? If so, this is God's path to blessing.

—∞∞—

Steady plodding brings prosperity (Proverbs 21:5 TLB).

If we eschew routine work, we're more likely to chase after phantom deals that are figments of our imagination. Be careful not to be led astray by fantasies that lead nowhere. No gimmick or conniving circumstance can replace hard work. Wisdom stops chasing after the next scheme and sticks instead to the certainty of available work. What does your spouse say is the smart thing to do? Give your spouse all the facts and then listen.

Working is easy when everything is going well and there is no threat of job loss or likelihood of increased responsibility with less pay. However, during uncertain times, Christ followers can step up and set the example. Your hope and hard work provide a testimony of trust in the

Lord. Stay engaged—execute your tasks with excellence, and you will inspire others in their labor of love.

See your routine work as your worship of the Lord. He is blessing your faithfulness to follow through with the smallest of details. Are you content to serve Christ in your current career? Work is your way to show the world your Savior. Excellence in what you do attracts attention to what Almighty God can do. He is your audience of one in your routine work.

―∞∞∞―

Whatever you do, work at it with all your heart, as working for the Lord, not for human masters, since you know that you will receive an inheritance from the Lord as a reward. It is the Lord Christ you are serving (Colossians 3:23-24).

Lord, in what ways can I reflect You in my everyday responsibilities at work?

Related Readings
Genesis 2:15; 1 Kings 19:19; Romans 12:11; 1 Timothy 4:11-12

37

Righteous Light

※

The light of the righteous shines brightly,
but the lamp of the wicked is snuffed out.

Proverbs 13:9

Righteousness shines the brightest when the days are darkest. We are called and compelled as Christians to glow for God during gloomy times. Are you caught up in our culture's chaos, or do you see a chance to burn brightly for Jesus? Hard times can harden our hearts or humble them, but broken hearts burn the brightest.

Jesus said, "Let your light shine before others, that they may see your good deeds and glorify your Father in heaven" (Matthew 5:16). Light left unattended extinguishes, but light exposed to the air of Almighty God's love continues to illuminate. Difficult days require you to depend on the Lord, and as a result, others can tell that your acts of service are energized by your faith. If you panic instead of praying, you will miss out on opportunities to love others.

※

We ought always to thank God for you, brothers and
sisters, and rightly so, because your faith is growing
more and more, and the love all of you have for
one another is increasing (2 Thessalonians 1:3).

I often ask, "In my uncertainty, am I so worried about my stuff that I miss the window of opportunity to serve others?" Shining the light may mean inviting someone to live in my home for a season, paying mortgage payments for a few months for a friend, volunteering at a local shelter, or increasing my gifts to the church. Righteous light shines the brightest when fueled by love.

Christ in us invites others to know Him. "For God, who said, 'Let light shine out of darkness,' made his light shine in our hearts to give us the light of the knowledge of God's glory displayed in the face of Christ" (2 Corinthians 4:6). Consider inviting some neighbors over for a six-week Bible study on money or marriage and watch what God does.

> Do everything without grumbling or arguing,
> so that you may become blameless and pure,
> children of God without fault in a warped and
> crooked generation. Then you will shine among
> them like stars in the sky (Philippians 2:14-15).

Who around me is suffering dark circumstances? How can I bring the light of Christ's love to them?

Related Readings
Job 18:5-6; Isaiah 50:10-11; Luke 11:36; Revelation 21:23

38

Dollar Cost Averaging

⎯⎯⎯⎯⎯⎯ ∾ ⎯⎯⎯⎯⎯⎯

Dishonest money dwindles away,
but he who gathers money little by little makes it grow.

Proverbs 13:11

Is there a method to your money management? Do you have a process in place to steadily save over time? If not, it is never too late to set up a system for saving. Some of us struggle with this because we bet on big returns, only to suffer loss. Steadily saving may not be as exciting as riskier investing, but it's much more secure. Finances can be a source of anxiety or an opportunity to demonstrate our faithfulness.

Get-rich-quick schemes only feed greed. In God's economy, those who diligently deposit smaller amounts in secure places reap rewards. Wise stewards give the first 10 percent of their income as a tithe to the heavenly Father, and they invest the second 10 percent in the future. Money obtained by vanity is spent on vanity, but money gained by hard work and honesty is retained for growth.

⎯⎯⎯ ∾ ⎯⎯⎯

Unless the LORD builds the house,
    the builders labor in vain.
Unless the LORD watches over the city,
    the guards stand watch in vain.
In vain you rise early
    and stay up late,
toiling for food to eat—
    for he grants sleep to those he loves
      (Psalm 127:1-2).

It takes discipline not to spend all our earnings. The advertising industry exploits our emotions. Culture entices us to spend not only all we have but even more than we have, so be on guard with a simple system for saving. For example, set up an automatic draft from each paycheck that goes straight into a savings account. Preserve this cash, and one day your financial fruit tree will become an orchard.

Look to the Lord as your provider, and remember that you are a steward of His stuff. Wise management of your Master's money includes saving. God wants your financial security to grow so you are free to give more and serve others. So we ask ourselves, "Am I frivolously spending just for today, or am I disciplined each day to deposit a dollar toward tomorrow?"

The plans of the diligent lead to profit
as surely as haste leads to poverty (Proverbs 21:5).

Lord, how would You have me manage Your money today and prepare for tomorrow?

Related Readings
Psalm 128:2; Jeremiah 17:11; Ephesians 4:28; James 5:1-5

39

Love Disciplines

———— ᙚ ————

Whoever spares the rod hates their children,
but the one who loves their children
is careful to discipline them.

Proverbs 13:24

L ove carefully disciplines, but apathy silently ignores. Love looks
for ways to instruct and improve, while busyness has no time for
a tender touch of truth. Do you take the time to discipline your children? Do your kids know your rebuke as well as your encouragement?
Because we love them, we correct their attitudes and challenge them
to better behavior. Rules restrain them from reacting foolishly or in
the flesh.

How can our children learn to make wise decisions if we do not
discipline them to love and obey God? Like warm lumps of clay in the
hands of a skilled artist, our children are moldable, and their character
is pliable in Christ's hands. We seek consistency in our own character so
we have the moral authority and respect to lead them. Your children's
first impression of the Lord comes from their father and mother, so be
an authority who reveals His love.

———— ᙚ ————

The living, the living—they praise you,
as I am doing today;
parents tell their children
about your faithfulness (Isaiah 38:19).

The branch of a tree is easily bent when it is tender, so when children are young, start training them to yield to Christ's lordship. "Start children off in the way they should go, and when they are old they will not turn from it" (Proverbs 22:6). Foolishness rejects faith and the prayerful punishment of loving parents. "Folly is bound up in the heart of a child, but the rod of discipline will drive it far away" (Proverbs 22:15). Discipline leads to freedom.

Your consistent concern for growth in your children's character invites their respect. "We have all had human fathers who disciplined us and we respected them for it" (Hebrews 12:9). Loving parents honestly inquire, "How do I respond to the Lord's discipline?" As my heavenly Father disciplines me and I grow as a result, I become an earthly father worth following.

---∞∞∞---

For whom the LORD loves He reproves,
Even as a father corrects the son in whom
he delights (Proverbs 3:12 NASB).

What area of my child's growth requires me to be more consistent in discipline?

Related Readings
Proverbs 23:13-14; 29:15-17; Hebrews 12:6-8; Ephesians 6:4

40

The Empty Nest

Where there are no oxen, the manger is empty,
but from the strength of an ox come abundant harvests.

Proverbs 14:4

Are you an empty nester? If you are, how does that make you feel?
Mad, sad, glad, lonely, without purpose, free...all these emotions
are common. You have raised your children well, and now they are on
their own. You are proud of them, but you miss them. They call from
college (especially daughters), but it is not the same. Exporting your
babies into adulthood is not easy, but this is their time to walk by faith
and know God for themselves.

We raise them the best we know how—with love, discipline, and
belief in Jesus Christ. Sometimes they frustrate us by not cleaning their
room. Like an animal in a barn, they can be messy and smelly. Some
days you want a little peace and quiet because they are angry and loud
and fighting with their siblings. But the empty nest is quiet. The kids
are nowhere to be found, so enjoy them while you can.

Train up a child in the way he should go,
And when he is old he will not depart
from it (Proverbs 22:6 NKJV).

You send them off to grow up and gain a heart of gratitude. By
God's grace they will visit with a new sense of appreciation and maturity. A little distance can help your friendship with your adult child to

grow. The space doesn't necessarily mean you will be taken for granted. It's harder to keep up and communicate, but in some ways it's more gratifying. You prepared them to leave your home and eventually cleave to the one the Lord has for them in marriage. Our empty nest is a test of our trust in God's plan.

Engage with your spouse in your empty nest. Do you feel as if you have drifted apart over the years? If so, intentionally rebuild intimacy with your best friend. Make these days of marriage your best—believe the Lord has given your lover to you so you can grow old together. Anticipate the gift of grandkids, as they will keep you busy and lively. The empty nest is a season to enjoy the fruit of your family.

A good person leaves an inheritance for
their children's children (Proverbs 13:22).

Lord, how can I best use the season of life I am in for Your kingdom purposes?

Related Readings
Genesis 7:1; Proverbs 31:15; Matthew 19:5; Acts 10:2

41

Self-Deception

*There is a way that appears to be right,
but in the end it leads to death.*

Proverbs 14:12

Self-deception is the worst kind of dishonesty because it is so con-vincing. Subtly it entices our mind and emotions to build on a lie. For example, self-deception whispers into the ear of our heart, "You are so smart and capable," but it forgets all about Christ's influence. Then we wander down a prayerless path, blazed in our own strength, only to discover we missed God's best by a mile.

In reality, we are only as prosperous as our Lord allows us to be. He makes our path straight and successful—according to His definition of success. "I instruct you in the way of wisdom and lead you along straight paths" (Proverbs 4:11). Which voice do you follow—your own or your Savior's? Perhaps His plan is for you to make less money and have more family time. Maybe He would have you turn down this pro-motion and trust Him for a better one in a different season.

The pride of your heart has deceived you (Obadiah 3).

We can talk ourselves into anything, especially as it relates to money. I can easily justify a new house, car, kitchen, set of furniture, floor cov-ering, or grill. But do I really need to upgrade, or would I better off to simply repair what I have? How can the Lord trust me with something newer if I have not been a good steward of what He has already given me? Trustworthy people can be trusted with more, but selfish or corrupt people miss out on opportunities. Manage your present possessions well.

Self-deceivers are self-destroyers, so avoid self-delusion by being accountable. Give others permission to ask you uncomfortable questions, even hard ones. Better to be embarrassed in private now than to be humiliated in public later. Humility invites loving friends to inspect our lives. You do much better when others provide loving accountability.

> The heart is hopelessly dark and deceitful,
>   a puzzle that no one can figure out.
> But I, GOD, search the heart
>   and examine the mind.
> I get to the heart of the human.
>   I get to the root of things.
> I treat them as they really are,
>   not as they pretend to be (Jeremiah 17:9 MSG).

Am I transparent with my money and motives? What do God and my godly advisors think?

Related Readings
Psalm 1:6; Isaiah 59:8; Matthew 7:13-14; Galatians 6:3

42

A Nation Exalted

⧟

Righteousness exalts a nation,
but sin condemns any people.

Proverbs 14:34

What makes a nation great? Its goodness—that's what God blesses. Righteousness is the platform the Lord uses to lift up a nation as an example for other nations to follow. However, like people, a nation can fall from God's grace. His blessing is removed when a haughty country shows no remorse for sin and even sanctions it. A blessed nation will cease to be great when it forgets where it came from by jettisoning Jesus.

It is when a nation is hurting that it needs healing the most. The nation of Israel experienced this. "If my people, who are called by my name, will humble themselves and pray and seek my face and turn from their wicked ways, then will I hear from heaven, and I will forgive their sin and will heal their land" (2 Chronicles 7:14). Have we drifted as a nation to not needing God? Has our sin found us out? Are we reaping what we have sown?

⧟

In that day you will say:
"Give praise to the Lord, proclaim his name;
    make known among the nations what he has done,
    and proclaim that his name is exalted" (Isaiah 12:4).

People don't sneak out of a blessed nation. They sneak in. People of the world flock to a country Christ has blessed. The best and the brightest are drawn to places where they can chase their dreams. Out of its goodness, a nation becomes a magnet for mankind. Righteousness reposes in the heart of a great nation, supporting virtue and suppressing vice.

A crippled country can make a comeback, but not without consequences. It starts with individuals repenting and taking responsibility for their actions. "How can I come clean with Christ?" "Have I been financially irresponsible?" "Has greed governed my giving?" "Has fear frozen my faith?" "Have comfort and ease become my idols?" The Lord exalts a nation that stays on its knees in dependence and awe of Almighty God.

He has declared that he will set you in praise, fame
and honor high above all the nations he has made
and that you will be a people holy to the LORD your
God, as he promised (Deuteronomy 26:19).

God, what do I need to do in order for You to trust our nation
again with greatness?

Related Readings
Proverbs 11:11; Jeremiah 22:2-25; Matthew 12:21; Romans 16:25-27

43

A Measured Response

—oɕɕɔ—

A gentle answer turns away wrath,
but a harsh word stirs up anger.

Proverbs 15:1

A knee-jerk reaction is a quick, unthinking, highly emotional re-response. People react in anger when they feel insulted. They withdraw when they feel left out. They react with gossip when they feel mistreated. They react defensively when they feel criticized. Reacting is easy because it doesn't require thought or consideration of boundaries. Hasty reactions are rarely helpful, so they often lead to regret. The flesh reacts, but the Spirit leads us to make measured responses.

To make a measured response, we must quiet our impulses and take time to cool down, think, and process the issue in prayer. When we receive an email that offends our pride or hurts our feelings, we refrain from firing back an immediate defense. We remind ourselves that email is helpful for transmitting information but not for communicating emotions. When a friend or family member makes a disrespectful remark about us at a social gathering, we wait a few days before we talk with them so we can respond with logic, not emotion. We discuss with them how to keep our relationship whole, not fractured.

—oɕɕɔ—

By long forbearance and calmness of spirit a judge
or ruler is persuaded, and soft speech breaks down
the most bonelike resistance (Proverbs 25:15 AMP).

When your blood pressure rises, pause and ask Christ to guard your heart with His peace. When your mind goes to a worst-case scenario, ask the Lord to renew your thinking so you can see the bigger picture of what He is doing behind the scenes. When your throat dries and your lips are parched, let the Holy Spirit flow from you with gracious words. When the hairs stand up on your arm, remember your heavenly Father knows the number of hairs on your head, so He can handle this event or person. Another's arrogance is agitating, but your humble response invites a calm conversation. Respond in love.

Jesus modeled a loving response in place of an angry reaction (John 7:20-24). He was accused of being demon possessed, but instead of insulting their ignorance, He appealed to their intellect by invoking their knowledge of Moses. And He went on to logically explain why it's okay to heal a broken body on the Sabbath. Indeed, Christ in us gives us a calm spirit to respond rationally and with respect. Our Spirit-led response will bear spiritual fruit. The Lord will use our soft answers to soften hearts that need the Savior. We pray they will respond to Jesus in saving faith.

Do not let any unwholesome talk come out of
your mouths, but only what is helpful for building
others up according to their needs, that it may
benefit those who listen (Ephesians 4:29).

Heavenly Father, give me pause to respond with respect and love, not in hasty judgment.

Related Readings
Ecclesiastes 10:4; Matthew 12:36; Ephesians 5:4; Colossians 3:8

44

Pursue Righteousness

The Lord detests the way of the wicked,
but he loves those who pursue righteousness.

Proverbs 15:9

What does it mean to pursue righteousness? We know how to pursue happiness or financial security. We may pursue a husband or wife, but what is the pursuit of righteousness?

Righteousness is a standard of behavior that God defines as morally right. We pursue righteousness when we determine to understand what the Scriptures outline as right and integrate that into our behavior. To pursue righteousness is to live intentionally.

The pursuit of righteousness begins with the pursuit of God, for He is the Righteous One. He detests the way of the wicked but loves those who pursue righteousness. He loves those who pursue Him for righteousness' sake. So we seek Him because we need Him to transform us into the likeness of His Son Jesus. We become like what we pursue.

The Righteous One takes note of the house
of the wicked
and brings the wicked to ruin (Proverbs 21:12).

God makes the path of the righteous smooth—not without bumps along the way, but with clear direction for living. Do you need to know God's will for school, marriage, or work? Pursue righteousness, and He will direct your steps. Don't worry and fret over distant steps. Instead, by faith, focus on the next step. "The path of the righteous is level; you, the Upright One, make the way of the righteous smooth" (Isaiah 26:7).

Without your Lord and Savior Jesus, your "righteous acts are like filthy rags" (Isaiah 64:6). Indeed, it is not what you do for Jesus but the work of His Spirit in and through you that produces the fruit of righteousness. Remain in Him, and He will make you righteous—not holier-than-thou, but humble and loving. You become whatever you pursue, so you are wise and loved by the Lord when you pursue righteousness.

Abide in Me, and I in you. As the branch cannot
bear fruit of itself, unless it abides in the vine, neither
can you, unless you abide in Me (John 15:4 NKJV).

How can I be more intentional about pursuing righteousness and abiding in Christ?

Related Readings
1 Chronicles 29:17; Psalm 1:6; 1 Timothy 6:11; 2 Timothy 2:22

45

A Happy Heart

*A happy heart makes the face cheerful,
but heartache crushes the spirit.*

Proverbs 15:13

A happy heart aligns with heaven's perspective. It is based on something much broader and nobler than current circumstances. A heart of delight is not in denial about difficulties, nor is it irresponsible regarding raw reality. Rather, it takes its cheer from Christ. People can encourage us, but Jesus provides eternal encouragement. "Do not let your hearts be troubled. You believe in God; believe also in me" (John 14:1).

A cheerful face is not proof that a heart is not hurting. You may very well be suffering painful rejection from divorce, job loss, or missed opportunity. However, the aching of a hopeful heart is accompanied by assurance anchored in Almighty God. Hurt need not exclude happiness. Go to Jesus for affirmation, and He will make your heart whole and happy.

Even in laughter the heart may ache,
and rejoicing may end in grief (Proverbs 14:13).

Sometimes your spirit is crushed in the moment you receive baffling information. Someone may treat you disrespectfully. You later learn of the deep wounds that person is carrying without Christ. Maybe a team member who is a loyal friend and confidant is moving on. You feel betrayed and alone. Use this loss to lead you toward the Lord's love and healing. Our loss is God's gain in governing our hearts.

The disciples felt loss and sorrow before the cross. Jesus discerned this and said, "You are filled with grief because I have said these things. But very truly I tell you, it is for your good that I am going away. Unless I go away, the Advocate will not come to you; but if I go, I will send him to you" (John 16:6-7). He is the emissary of eternal happiness. A happy heart is full of faith in the Lord. Peer into the face of Christ, and you will go away with a cheerful countenance. Follow His commands and find joy.

❄

> The precepts of the LORD are right,
>   giving joy to the heart.
> The commands of the LORD are radiant,
>   giving light to the eyes (Psalm 19:8).

Is my heart fully controlled by the Holy Spirit? Am I happy and content in Christ?

Related Readings

Nehemiah 2:2; Proverbs 12:25; Acts 27:25-36; 2 Corinthians 2:7

46

Holy Spirit Motivated

———— ✾ ————

All a person's ways seem innocent to him,
but motives are weighed by the LORD.

Proverbs 16:2

Why do you do what you do? Is it for the glory of God or for personal satisfaction? There is a subtle difference in serving the Lord for His glory and doing our own thing, only mentioning Him as an afterthought. We cannot impartially judge our hearts, but Christ can. We are too close to objectively assess our actions and motives. However, the Holy Spirit has an effective way to weigh what we do.

Sometimes His way does not make sense. He has you in a fruitful situation, and then the Holy Spirit leads you to serve discouraged disciples who have overwhelming needs. "The Spirit told Philip, 'Go to that chariot and stay near it'…Philip baptized him. When they came up out of the water, the Spirit of the Lord suddenly took Philip away, and the eunuch did not see him again, but went on his way rejoicing" (Acts 8:29,38-39). Are you willing to leave a place where you are loved and take on a new initiative with plenty of unknowns? Is your heart in it for Him and what is best for the kingdom, or is it about making your name known?

———— ✾ ————

By faith Abraham, when called to go to a
place he would later receive as his inheritance,
obeyed and went, even though he did not
know where he was going (Hebrews 11:8).

Jesus experienced this before His intense temptation with the devil. "Jesus, full of the Holy Spirit, left the Jordan and was led by the Spirit into the wilderness, where for forty days he was tempted by the devil" (Luke 4:1-2). Sometimes God leads us through the desert of temptation to purify our motives. When He eventually delivers us from our adversity, we can lift up a praise offering to Him. Indeed, our gratitude to God gives Him the glory.

In reality, only God really knows your real motivation. The Holy Spirit can provide the motivation you need to sustain your service. Be like the captain of a ship, who serves for the sake of the crew and to keep the pirates at bay. Ask yourself, "Am I willing to do what I do without pay or for lesser pay for a period of time, or is money my true motive?" Begin each project with pure prayers inspired by the Holy Spirit. Motive matters most to your Master.

When you ask, you do not receive, because you
ask with wrong motives, that you may spend
what you get on your pleasures (James 4:3).

Can I be content when I receive only the consolation of Christ for my efforts?

Related Readings
Deuteronomy 9:4; 1 Samuel 16:7; Luke 16:15; 2 Corinthians 10:12

47

Moral Authority

⸺⸺⸺∞⸺⸺⸺

Kings detest wrongdoing,
for a throne is established through righteousness.

Proverbs 16:12

Moral authority gives leaders the creditability to lead effectively. Presidents, judges, congressmen, governors, mayors, businessmen, teachers, preachers, and parents all require moral authority to be leaders worth following. A person's faith in God's standard bolsters respect from his or her followers. So what is your standard for conduct? Is your conscience governed by Christ's character? Is He your baseline of behavior?

When "everyone [does] what [is] right in his own eyes" (Judges 21:25 NKJV), the results are cultural chaos and moral confusion. This is true in the workplace that is inconsistent in its accountability, and also in a home environment where the parents do not model the behavior they expect from their children. People are motivated to follow rules consistently when they know the leaders have established them in righteousness.

⸺⸺∞⸺⸺

Who is wise and understanding among you? Let
them show it by their good life, by deeds done in
the humility that comes from wisdom (James 3:13).

Our Creator has given us wisdom and direction based on His righteous standard of behavior. If, however, we don't live with integrity, we forfeit these gifts. God's gift of freedom flourishes only in a faith-based society. Those who are ungrateful to God travel down a path of pride to their peril. "There is a way that seems right to a man, but its end is the way of death" (Proverbs 16:25 NKJV). Moral authority is accountable to Almighty God.

Therefore, I have to ask myself, "Do I detest wrongdoing? Do I stand up to injustice with Christlike character? Do I compromise God's standards, or do I walk away from unseemly situations and shady deals?" The conscience of a culture changes one heart at a time. Moral authority is the master of a leader's fate. With it comes creditability and the Lord's blessing. Without it, we are left with a shell of service at best, corruption at worst.

---◦◊◦---

Those who have served well gain an excellent
standing and great assurance in their faith
in Christ Jesus (1 Timothy 3:13).

Do I lead with the moral authority of my Master Jesus?

Related Readings
2 Samuel 23:3-4; 2 Chronicles 19:5-7; Luke 12:48; Revelation 19:11

48

Pride Before Destruction

∽∾∾

Pride goes before destruction,
a haughty spirit before a fall.

Proverbs 16:18

Pride is an entrée to destructive behavior. It facilitates foolish actions and undermines relationships. Pride is not afraid to offend anyone and appeases no one. Its demanding spirit may gain short-term results under duress, but in the long term, people loathe its indulgent attitude. Indeed, do not fear pride in others; fear it in yourself.

False humility is a subtle form of pride. "Do not let anyone who delights in false humility and the worship of angels disqualify you. Such a person also goes into great detail about what they have seen; they are puffed up with idle notions by their unspiritual mind" (Colossians 2:18). These are people who use spiritual talk to try to impress others with religious information. False humility speaks softly about its superior spiritual knowledge.

However, heaven is not idle in its attitude toward pride. It is pride that hurled Lucifer out of the presence of the Lord and into hell (see Isaiah 14:11-13). God runs out of patience with those who are proud of heart and set in their ways. He brings down the stubborn and insubordinate. Pride forgets God and marginalizes faith, so He removes the self-absorbed.

∽∾∾

Before a downfall the heart is haughty,
but humility comes before honor (Proverbs 18:12).

Therefore, humble yourself before God and man. Engage in extending and receiving forgiveness. Give Christ the credit for your accomplishments, and take responsibility for your failures. Humility honestly asks, "Do I care more about serving others than indulging myself? Am I a generous giver or a greedy getter?" Replace haughtiness with humility, and the Lord will lift you up.

For all those who exalt themselves will
be humbled, and those who humble
themselves will be exalted (Luke 14:11).

Do I use my influence to further the success of others or to advance my own agenda?

Related Readings
Leviticus 26:19; 2 Chronicles 26:16; Daniel 5:20; Luke 1:51

49

The Test of Trust

The crucible for silver and the furnace for gold,
but the LORD tests the heart.

Proverbs 17:3

The Lord tests our hearts to build our trust. Resistance to our effort creates a reason to reach out to our Creator. Your test of trust is not a trivial pursuit but a process of purification. Just as the silversmith uses the cleansing crucible to purify his precious metal, the Lord uses tests to extract our pride and replace it with His humility. Tests invite trust.

Indeed, the fruit of refining trials is faith. Perhaps you are facing a financial test. Will you spend less and give more as you watch your net worth shrink? You may have failed the relational test in your marriage, with your children, or with a parent. Be hopeful, for you can find success in failure. Failure strips away the nonessentials so all that is left is raw faith. Failure is not final. It is a stepping-stone for the Lord's work.

For you, God, tested us;
you refined us like silver (Psalm 66:10).

Testing is the Lord's tool to teach you to trust. You may feel humiliated and exposed, as if the Holy Spirit had strip-searched your soul. Refinement is not always pleasant, but it is necessary to prepare you for success at work and home. Christ builds your character to prepare you for your next milestone of achievement. Fire fuels faith.

In the end, affluence may be your greatest test of trust in God. The more you have, the less you feel you need the Lord. "You may say to yourself, 'My power and the strength of my hands have produced this wealth for me.' But remember the LORD your God, for it is he who gives you the ability to produce wealth" (Deuteronomy 8:17-18).

Have I passed the test of prosperity? Do I give Christ the credit for my accomplishments?

Related Readings
2 Chronicles 32:21; Job 23:10; 1 Corinthians 3:13; 1 Peter 1:7

50

The Gift of Grandchildren

Children's children are a crown to the aged,
and parents are the pride of their children.

Proverbs 17:6

There are privileges to maturing in age, and one of them is the gift of grandchildren. Like a monarch's crown, their exceptional value is to be displayed proudly. When you look at their hands and feet, you pray for them to handle life prayerfully and to walk wisely with the Lord. When you gaze into their innocent eyes, you see glimpses of God's glory. You pray for them to look often to the face of Jesus and receive His love.

Grandchildren are gifts from God that invite love and unify families. They are reminders that the Lord is at work extending His legacy. So as you love these little ones, make sure to plant the Word of God in their hearts, modeling grace, love, forgiveness, and the fear of the Lord. Teach them to keep their eyes on Jesus because He will never let them down. Godly grandparents invite their grandchildren into their lives.

May you live to see your children's children—
peace be on Israel (Psalm 128:6).

Invite them to your work so they can see how you relate to people with patience, encouragement, and accountability. Invite them into your home so they soak in your unconditional love and learn respect for their grandmother and grandfather. Make sure they catch you laughing out loud every time they visit with you. Call them on the phone, send them emails and birthday cards, take them on trips, and buy them ice cream, clothes, and their first Bible. Make sure their memories with you bring smiles to their faces.

If you are a parent, honor your parents by helping them to make memories with your children. Take a break from parenting and let your mom and dad spoil them. If you are a grandparent, be extremely grateful to your children for the opportunity to invest in their children. Honor your children by respecting their way of parenting. Work with them, not against them. Indeed, your children still need your time, money, and wisdom.

From everlasting to everlasting
    the Lord's love is with those who fear him,
        and his righteousness with their children's children—
with those who keep his covenant
    and remember to obey his precepts
        (Psalm 103:17-18).

How can I be intentional in my time with my grandchildren? Or how can I help my parents create wonderful memories with my children?

Related Readings
Psalms 78:4-6; 128:6; Proverbs 13:22; Joel 1:2-4

51

Foolish Children

∞∞

To have a fool for a child brings grief;
there is no joy for the parent of a godless fool.

Proverbs 17:21

Foolish children flail around trying to find themselves. They are often terrible at managing money because they have no concept of conservative spending and consistent saving. They look to Mom and Dad to bail them out. They want their parents to provide for them without implementing a plan for accountability. Childish children become masters of manipulation and guilt, saying, "If you really loved me…"

This grieves the heart of their parents, who want to do the right thing but aren't sure what is right. The dad may be firm and the mom more merciful, so they must find a unified approach to loving their rebellious child. They cannot allow Satan to drive a wedge of doubt between them. Jesus said, "Every city or household divided against itself will not stand" (Matthew 12:25).

∞∞

> A wise son brings joy to his father,
>   but a foolish son brings grief to his mother
>   (Proverbs 10:1).

Start with sincere and aggressive prayer for a loved one bound up in foolish behavior. Pray for the Lord to change *you*, giving you the grace and courage to offer an aggressive love based on the love of your heavenly Father. You can love the unlovely as you ought only after receiving His unconditional love. Remember the joy you had when your child came into this world as God's gift. Trust their Creator to bring them back to Christ. He can.

Lastly, confide in the Christian community regarding your sorrow and hurt. You may be surprised to discover how many have suffered a similar fate. Move beyond the mistakes of the past and focus on faith in the present. Turn your child over to the Lord's love and discipline. Pray your foolish child will grow tired of folly and return to faith in God. Thus, in hope of a celebration one day, you can pray, "Christ, give me confidence to let them go and give them to You." Foolish children especially need the faithful prayers and love of their parents.

———— ∞∞ ————

"This son of mine was dead and is alive
again; he was lost and is found." So they
began to celebrate (Luke 15:24).

Lord, help me to see my child like You see me, Your child—with patient love and compassion.

Related Readings
2 Samuel 18:33; Proverbs 19:13-26; 2 Corinthians 2:3-4; 3 John 1:4

52

Strong and Secure

---◦◦◦---

The name of the LORD is a fortified tower;
the righteous run to it and are safe.

Proverbs 18:10

The Lord is strong and secure. Satan and his demons cannot scale His fortress. Our own fear is unable to undermine God's protection of us. Our Savior Jesus Christ is not scared in the face of unholy alliances. His name is sufficient for the saints, for there is nowhere else to go, as the apostle Peter declared. "Lord, to whom shall we go? You have the words of eternal life. We have come to believe and to know that you are the Holy One of God" (John 6:68-69).

So where do you go when you get frustrated and afraid? Do you have a safe place where you are sure to find wisdom and discernment? Or do you flounder in your faith, moving from one false hope to another, only to come up short and disillusioned? Pastors can declare the Word of God, but they are not 100 percent reliable as righteous resources. Employers who provide for our financial needs are instruments of the Lord, but they are not always consistent sources. Family and friends care, but they are not always there.

Only the Lord longs to always walk with you. Jesus said, "Surely I am with you always, to the very end of the age" (Matthew 28:20).

His name is a strong tower, so you can find rest and refuge in Him when doubts and fears rise up against you. Run to His righteous resting place for renewal and strength. This world saps our energy and endangers our soul, but Jesus brings us life. He is your strong tower, and He can restore your trust and peace.

God is more than able to take care of your every need. His tower of trust is impregnable and impenetrable. Go inside and stay awhile in intimacy with Him. Then go back into the world, clothed in your battle fatigues of faith. You are strong and secure in the trustworthy tower of your Lord Jesus. Be confident in Christ and His amazing grace.

—❦—

Finally, be strong in the Lord and in his mighty power.
Put on the full armor of God, so that you can take your
stand against the devil's schemes (Ephesians 6:10-11).

Do I seek my Savior's security in the tower of trust in Him? Am I clothed in Christ's character and power, ready to engage the world?

Related Readings
1 Samuel 17:45; Psalm 9:9-10; Matthew 1:23; Revelation 1:8

53

Overcoming an Offense

⚬⚭⚬

A brother wronged is more unyielding
than a fortified city;
disputes are like the barred gates of a citadel.

Proverbs 18:19

What happens when you offend another? How do you deal with the awkwardness? You probably feel embarrassed and regret saying or doing something that has weakened or even severed the relationship. However difficult, there is a process of penetrating hurt feelings and healing the heart. The Lord's desire is for us to first work out relational differences on earth and then reconcile with heaven. The words of Jesus are clear.

> If you enter your place of worship and, about to make an offering, you suddenly remember a grudge a friend has against you, abandon your offering, leave immediately, go to this friend and make things right. Then and only then, come back and work things out with God (Matthew 5:23-24 MSG).

An offense is a huge obstacle, especially when you are ignorant of its occurrence. But ignorance is not an excuse.

⚬⚭⚬

My son, if you have put up security for your neighbor,
if you have shaken hands in pledge for a stranger,
you have been trapped by what you said,

> ensnared by the words of your mouth.
> So do this, my son, to free yourself,
>   since you have fallen into your neighbor's hands:
> Go—to the point of exhaustion—
>   and give your neighbor no rest!
> Allow no sleep to your eyes,
>   no slumber to your eyelids.
> Free yourself, like a gazelle from the hand of the hunter,
>   like a bird from the snare of the fowler (Proverbs 6:1-5).

When you approach an offended friend, be careful not to say, "I'm sorry if I offended you." Instead, own it by confessing, "I'm so sorry I offended you." Though your offense may have been unintended, taking responsibility with humility and grace opens the door for forgiveness. Be patient, for his or her guard is up, and it will take time for a grudge to go away. Continue to slay the offended friend with severe kindness. Unconditional love lingers long.

Reconciled differences become hopeful examples to others who face similarly strained relationships. Pursue your insulted friend as Jesus pursued you—with unrelenting love. He said, "The Son of Man came to seek and to save the lost" (Luke 19:10). Persistent prayer and love melt away the cold bars of an offended heart.

> Therefore confess your sins to each other and pray for
> each other so that you may be healed (James 5:16).

How can I humble myself and own what I did? Have I clearly confessed my sin and asked for forgiveness? Am I contributing to the healing process?

Related Readings

Genesis 27:41-45; Proverbs 16:32; Amos 1:11-12; 2 Timothy 2:22

54

A Wife's Blessing

⁓ɬ∞

*He who finds a wife finds what is good
and receives favor from the LORD.*

Proverbs 18:22

Why is a wife good for a man? How does she bless him? She is good for her husband because she complements and completes him. She is the beauty, and he is the beast. She is finesse, and he is forceful. She is mercy, and he is the protector. She is elegant, and he is earthy. She works on her hands, and he works with his hands. A wife brings life and love to the longings of the one she loves. She is good for a man because this is God's plan.

A good wife is a righteous remedy for loneliness. "The LORD God said, 'It is not good for the man to be alone. I will make a helper suitable for him'" (Genesis 2:18). A man needs help because by himself he lacks the discernment to make the wisest decisions. Alone he is okay, but with the right wife he is elevated to excellence. She facilitates faithfulness to God. She prays for her husband's full potential to be realized and enjoyed.

⁓ɬ∞

> May your fountain be blessed,
> and may you rejoice in the wife of your youth
> (Proverbs 5:18).

A man finds the right wife through prayer and patience. He waits on the Lord to lead him to a woman of character whose life is attractive because she loves Jesus Christ more than her future husband. She is not overly needy, as she is loved by her heavenly Father in a wholesome and healthy way. Since she is full of grace, she is able to give grace. She is like a hidden jewel, and a wise man will cherish and value a woman of this quality as his wife.

"The kingdom of heaven is like treasure hidden in a field. When a man found it, he hid it again, and then in his joy went and sold all he had and bought that field" (Matthew 13:44). Praise the Lord when you find the right wife. She is a gift from God to be honored and served. Tell her how blessed you are to be her husband.

In the same way, you husbands must give honor to your wives. Treat your wife with understanding as you live together. She may be weaker than you are, but she is your equal partner in God's gift of new life. Treat her as you should so your prayers will not be hindered (1 Peter 3:7 NLT).

How can I show gratitude to my wife? Do I thank God for her daily, praying for her to feel my love for her?

Related Readings
Genesis 24:44-67; Psalm 128:3; Luke 1:30; 1 Corinthians 7:2

55

Wisdom Yields Patience

━━━━━━━━━━━━ ∽∾ ━━━━━━━━━━━━

A person's wisdom yields patience;
it is to one's glory to overlook an offense.

Proverbs 19:11

Wisdom brings out patience in a willing soul. We can practice forbearance when we understand and appreciate another person's perspective. Patience gives the benefit of the doubt and waits on pronouncing judgment. Why does wisdom wait? She learns to wait because she knows that rash responses lead to messy consequences. "Do you see someone who speaks in haste? There is more hope for a fool than for them" (Proverbs 29:20).

Discretion is able to defer anger until all sides give their perspective. It does not react to part of the truth, but patiently extracts all the evidence. Discretion is protection against pride's harsh judgment and guards over a heart becoming gullible. "Discretion will protect you, and understanding will guard you" (Proverbs 2:11). Learn to love people despite their imperfections, and you will help them grow into perfection. Assume the best.

What does it mean to overlook an offense? It is a Spirit-led response that practices real-time forgiveness. Rather than focusing on the offense, you choose to create an environment of grace in which you can reach out to see what's behind the offender's words or actions. Often people have a hurting heart that has never been healed, and just as if they had a sore spot on their body, they recoil when people bump up against it. Your joy or success may have rubbed against a raw spot of rejection on their soul.

Therefore, wisdom has compassion for an estranged soul and prays for its return to the Lord's refuge of acceptance, love, and wholeness. Love is a universal language for those languishing in their faith. Love "always protects, always trusts, always hopes, always perseveres" (1 Corinthians 13:7). Wisdom gives us the patience we need to respond to offenses with love and forgiveness.

How can I give a wise and patient response when I'm offended? What current offense can I overlook with forgiveness, love, and acceptance?

Related Readings
1 Chronicles 22:12; Ecclesiastes 7:9; Matthew 5:21-26,38-45; Romans 12:18-21

56

Be Kind to the Poor

⎯⎯⎯⎯⎯ ⟳ ⎯⎯⎯⎯⎯

Whoever is kind to the poor lends to the LORD,
and he will reward them for what they have done.

Proverbs 19:17

We can lend to the Lord by being kind to the poor. What does it mean to lend to the Lord? It means extending the Almighty's active, loving concern for the poor and needy. Christ covers their debt with interest, and He extends rewards back to the generous giver. This demonstrates the priority of loving "the least of these" in Jesus's name. When we extend kindness to those in severe need, we are serving the Lord Himself. You see Jesus in their hopeful eyes, just as He described.

> I was hungry and you gave me something to eat, I was thirsty and you gave me something to drink, I was a stranger and you invited me in, I needed clothes and you clothed me, I was sick and you looked after me, I was in prison and you came to visit me...Truly I tell you, whatever you did for one of the least of these brothers and sisters of mine, you did for me (Matthew 25:35-36,40).

Serving the poor is serving the Lord.

Perhaps you start by praying for the poor. Choose a time of the week and listen to the Lord's extreme love for the least of these. He may lead you to serve precious poor children by volunteering at an after-school program. He may nudge you to give a day a week to go downtown and help the homeless—serve in the soup kitchen, organize clothes—all the while sharing the good news of Jesus with a smile and encouraging Scripture.

The Lord rewards kindness to the poor. Your reward may be the simple satisfaction of obeying Christ's command. It may be the fulfillment of seeing your family's faith lived out in a practical, hands-on opportunity. It may be the joy of seeing someone receive the Savior you modeled. The Bible teaches the motivation of giving in love—"If I give all I possess to the poor and give over my body to hardship that I may boast, but do not have love, I gain nothing" (1 Corinthians 13:3).

Whom can I regularly join in prayer for the impoverished? Where does the Lord want me to be kind to the poor on His behalf?

Related Readings
2 Samuel 12:6; Isaiah 58:10; Galatians 2:10; James 2:15-16

57

Avoid Enablement

⎯⎯⎯⎯ ∞ ⎯⎯⎯⎯

A hot-tempered person must pay the penalty;
rescue them, and you will have to do it again.

Proverbs 19:19

Watching someone fail is painful. However, failure may be what the person needs to eventually experience success. When we prematurely intervene in someone's problem, we can unknowingly prolong the pain. Short-term relief can short-circuit long-term solutions. Do you know someone who needs your prayers but not your solutions? Resist the temptation to rush in and rescue. Trust that God is at work and that He will work it out.

We are shortsighted if we think we can be people's savior when they actually need to depend on their only Savior, Jesus Christ. Perhaps they are victims of drug and alcohol addiction. Their condition may have to worsen before they get better. When we are at the bottom, we have nowhere to look but up. The Lord lifts up the broken.

⎯⎯⎯⎯ ∞ ⎯⎯⎯⎯

He lifted me out of the slimy pit,
   out of the mud and mire;
he set my feet on a rock
   and gave me a firm place to stand (Psalm 40:2).

Anger is especially hard to tame unless there is brokenness in the presence of God and man. Hotheaded behavior justifies its actions with feelings of rejection, self-pity, and hurt. It is a heart issue that only heaven can heal. Your sympathy is simply a surface salve. The broken person's wholeness will come through confession, repentance, and taking responsibility. Angry people must suffer the painful consequences of their actions, or they will be perpetual offenders.

The best way to help people who have lost their way is to listen and love without enabling their bad behavior. They need your wisdom much more than your money. Writing a check is easier than engaging in passionate prayer for their soul. Money can mask their need for real resolution. Let them go, and let God heal them.

—∞∞—

Jesus looked at him and loved him. "One thing
you lack," he said. "Go, sell everything you have
and give to the poor, and you will have treasure in
heaven. Then come, follow me" (Mark 10:21).

How can I offer tough love and trust God? Whom do I need to stop enabling so they can take responsibility?

Related Readings
1 Samuel 20:30-31; Proverbs 22:24-25; 1 Corinthians 13:5; James 1:20

58

On Purpose

The purposes of a person's heart are deep waters,
but one who has insight draws them out.

Proverbs 20:5

What is your unique purpose? Do you live uniquely you, or are you fulfilling a role you really resent? One way to get at these questions is to ask yourself, "What does my Savior Jesus expect of me?" Christ has clearly pronounced His purposes. "For we are God's handiwork, created in Christ Jesus to do good works, which God prepared in advance for us to do" (Ephesians 2:10). The Lord has already laid out your plan of rewarding activities on His behalf.

Start by examining your passions—not just what excites you, but what roles you are willing to persevere in even when you suffer. Vocational ministry may seem noble, but can you forgive in the face of rejection, and can you serve without people's recognition and affirmation? A minister's purpose is to remain a faithful servant of Jesus Christ. "I thank Christ Jesus our Lord who has enabled me, because He counted me faithful, putting me into the ministry" (1 Timothy 1:12 NKJV). He chooses us for His purposes and glory.

Indeed, each season of life is defined by a new set of purposes. When you are single, you lay a foundation of financial and moral responsibility. When you are married, you prepare for a family and develop friendships with people in a similar season of life. When you have children, you serve and teach the ways of God. When you are an empty nester, you enjoy your spouse, mentor younger believers, and aggressively invest in the kingdom of God.

Above all, get before God and allow Him to define your purposes. Then stay "on purpose" with the focused disciplines of prayer and execution. If you're a teacher, teach; if you're a student, study. If you're a mom, mother; or a dad, father. If you're a leader, lead; or an artist, create. Whatever you do, become the best you can be before God and man.

—⊗⊗⊗—

They did what your power and will had decided
beforehand should happen (Acts 4:28).

Am I "on purpose," or do I need to adjust my actions? Do my passions, gifts, and skills align around a common purpose, all for God's glory?

Related Readings
Proverbs 18:4; Jeremiah 29:11-13; Hebrews 3:1-6; 1 Corinthians 2:11

59

Marvelously Made

———— ∞ ————

Ears that hear and eyes that see—
the LORD *has made them both.*

Proverbs 20:12

Our bodies are marvelously made, which means we have a marvelous Maker. How could such precision and complexity exist without a supreme Creator in Christ? The human body is grand evidence for Almighty God. We are created by God, and we are created for God. The Almighty is the architect of our flesh, so our actions reflect Him. "Does he who fashioned the ear not hear? Does he who formed the eye not see?" (Psalm 94:9).

Our feet are designed to walk by faith down familiar and unfamiliar paths of righteousness. Our eyes look to eternity, always aware of our accountability before the Almighty. Our ears listen to the voice of the Holy Spirit and obey His commands. Our hands are quick to serve others in the name of Jesus Christ. Your body is a billboard for belief in the Lord, so take care to present Christ with correct and consistent conduct.

———— ∞ ————

I praise you because I am fearfully and
wonderfully made;
your works are wonderful,
I know that full well (Psalm 139:14).

Every muscle, nerve, and fiber of our being is bold to proclaim praise to its Creator for His creation. In wonder and awe, we worship

God and give thanks for His grand plan, the body. As you witness the gestation of life in the womb of a loved one, your instincts feel instructed by God. He originates life and determines death. My heavenly Father has fashioned and formed all the parts of my frame.

Therefore, exclaim with adoration and thanksgiving to God for the beauty of His beings. Your body is a testament to the truth of His existence. Use it to point others to Jesus. Abuse it, and you poorly manage your Maker's physical phenomena. Your body is a bold exclamation of eternal consequences.

––––⌘––––

Blessed are your eyes because they see, and
your ears because they hear (Matthew 13:16).

How can I use my body in a way that helps others better understand Christ? Does my body take me to places and people that are pleasing to Him?

Related Readings
Psalm 119:18; Proverbs 18:15; Acts 26:18; Ephesians 1:17-18

60

Words of Worth

⚬⚬⚬

Gold there is, and rubies in abundance,
but lips that speak knowledge are a rare jewel.

Proverbs 20:15

Words of worth are rare jewels, waiting to be discovered by prayerful souls. God has placed some people in your life whose language is laced with His instructions. These trusting, tried-and-true servants of Christ are the ones you need to hear from often. They may be your parents, grandparents, teachers, clergy, sibling, spouse, child, or mentors, and their insights and understanding are at your disposal. Do you take the time to mine truth from their minds?

Avoid those whose trivial pursuit is primarily shallow conversations around current events. Instead, hang out with insightful saints who have a hold on heaven. Your mind and heart become rich in the resources of God when you obtain knowledge from His humble and wise followers. They do not announce their presence with fanfare, but you know they have been in the presence of the Father because their words are rich and robust.

Carriers of knowledge can be rich or poor, young or old, minority or majority, city or country, educated or uneducated.

Valuable speech is more than just a transfer of information. It is transformational truth spoken from a humble heart and a teachable mind. Words grow in their worth with those who remain students. So seek out learners who lean on the Lord and not their own understanding. The Holy Spirit instructs hungry hearts.

Use your own words to encourage, instruct, correct, and rebuke those you influence. Pray daily for a seeking soul you can generously give a gold nugget of wisdom, a ruby of reality, or a pearl of perception. Words are not to be wasted in worry. They are an investment from intimacy with God and instruction with man.

Do not let any unwholesome talk come out of your mouths, but only what is helpful for building others up according to their needs, that it may benefit those who listen (Ephesians 4:29).

Whose wise words can I learn from today? To whom can I extend kindness and knowledge today?

Related Readings

Job 28:12-19; Proverbs 25:12; Ecclesiastes 12:9-11; Romans 10:17-18

61

Divinely Directed

The king's heart is a stream of water in
the hand of the LORD;
he turns it wherever he will.

Proverbs 21:1 ESV

The Lord's hand directs the heart of a man or woman as if He were tracing the curvy course of a river. The ride may seem rough at times and even feel dangerous, but Providence leads wherever He pleases. Enjoy the ride and don't be overwhelmed by circumstances out of your control. The Lord's leadership in your life is a great adventure full of faith and uncertainty. The Holy Spirit is your guide, so go with Him, and you will travel well.

You may be depending on someone else to facilitate an opportunity for advancement. You don't have to fret, because God has their heart in the palm of His hand. Artaxerxes, king of Persia, asked his Jewish servant Nehemiah what he needed, and through this faithless but powerful and resourceful leader the Lord provided everything Nehemiah required to rebuild the walls of Jerusalem. "And because the gracious hand of my God was upon me, the king granted my requests" (Nehemiah 2:8).

You can be at peace with God's provision. It may not originate where you expect, but you can be certain nothing can cease the supply of Christ's endless endowment. Your eternal resources never run their course. When you live in the will of God, you will receive everything you need to carry out His assignment. Pray for favor from an influencer over the area in which you need assistance. Show up when asked, and then speak boldly on behalf of God. "They were all filled with the Holy Spirit and spoke the word of God with boldness" (Acts 4:31).

Lastly, look to the Lord, who can change men's minds to serve His purposes. In your own strength, you feel powerless to affect much-needed outcomes, but in His power the results are staggering. Waiting on God's directive is better than striving without Him.

The Lord longs to be gracious to you;
>   therefore he will rise up to show you compassion.
For the Lord is a God of justice.
>   Blessed are all who wait for him! (Isaiah 30:18).

Whom can I pray for, that the Lord will direct their heart? And what does God want to place in my heart for His purposes?

Related Readings
Ezra 7:27; Proverbs 20:24; Acts 7:10; Revelation 17:17

62

A Season of Separation

————— ∞ —————

*Better to live on a corner of the roof
than share a house with a quarrelsome wife.*

Proverbs 21:9

S ometimes a husband and wife need a season of separation, working
toward reconciliation as the ultimate outcome. Things have got-
ten so bad that hatred has a hold on the home. Couples who do not
communicate and who chronically agitate one another are not healthy.
Love and respect have been lost at the altar of anger and ego. They need
a revival of their original marriage vows to love unselfishly, for love
"does not dishonor others, it is not self-seeking, it is not easily angered,
it keeps no record of wrongs" (1 Corinthians 13:5).

You may be tolerating one another while the children are home, but
covertly you both have an exit strategy once you have an empty nest.
Do you really want to live this way? Is this honoring to the Lord, your
children, and your marriage? If your relationship suffers from the can-
cer of caustic conversation, take measures now to remove its deadly
influence. If you ignore this disease, it will eat away your character,
influence, peace, and joy.

Pride is the largest single contributor to a contentious relationship.
Neither party wants to take responsibility for their role in the marriage.
Blame never rebuilt a marriage. But words like these can go a long way:
"I'm sorry," "Please forgive me," "I was wrong," "Let's work this out."

Separation is meant to give you space to experience God's grace
and then relentlessly extend it back to your spouse. "Do not deprive
each other except perhaps by mutual consent and for a time, so that

you may devote yourselves to prayer. Then come together again so that Satan will not tempt you because of your lack of self-control" (1 Corinthians 7:5).

Satan would like to take you from separation to divorce, but your Savior specializes in reconciliation. Each of you is to humble yourself and come clean with Christ so you can be reunited in love and forgiveness. Allow the Lord to love you so you can love like Him, bold and beautiful. Wounded couples can rebuild a home of humility and happiness.

Be completely humble and gentle; be patient,
bearing with one another in love (Ephesians 4:2).

Am I willing to let go of my demands and replace them with acceptance and love?

Related Readings
Proverbs 12:4; 15:17; Acts 10:9; 1 John 4:11

63

The Pursuit of Pleasure

~∞~

Whoever loves pleasure will become poor;
whoever loves wine and oil will never be rich.

Proverbs 21:17

The pursuit of pleasure leads to poverty. When people search for pleasure without considering eternal values, they become poorly principled, poor with people, poor in soul, and poor managers of God's provision. Pleasure without a greater purpose produces a lame life. However, earthly enjoyments wed with God's will open up the windows of heaven. "He made known to us the mystery of his will according to his good pleasure, which he purposed in Christ" (Ephesians 1:9). His pleasure is good.

Pleasure is not evil, but when it overshadows our devotion to Christ, it is downright dangerous. The apostle Paul said we will live with this tension in the last days.

> But mark this: There will be terrible times in the last days. People will be lovers of themselves, lovers of money, boastful, proud, abusive, disobedient to their parents, ungrateful, unholy, without love, unforgiving, slanderous, without self-control, brutal, not lovers of the good, treacherous, rash, conceited, *lovers of pleasure rather than lovers of God*—having a form of godliness but denying its power (2 Timothy 3:1-5).

The Lord is not suggesting a both/and approach to loving Him and pursuing pleasure, but rather an either/or outlook. We choose to love

Christ or to amuse ourselves to death. Luxurious living without the Lord is vain and unfulfilling. Make pleasure subservient to serving your Savior, and you will find fulfillment and peace. For example, retreat to the beach or mountains to find pleasure in God's creation while enjoying Him and those you love. To enjoy your temporal life on earth to the fullest, focus on obeying heaven's eternal expectations.

Find pleasure where your heavenly Father finds pleasure. "His pleasure is not in the strength of the horse, nor his delight in the legs of the warrior; the LORD delights in those who fear him, who put their hope in his unfailing love" (Psalm 147:10-11). His pleasure is for us to do His good pleasure, which includes humble trust and submission to Him (Matthew 11:25-27). Therefore, take pleasure in Him.

How can I pursue the Lord's pleasures?

Related Readings
Proverbs 10:23; Ephesians 1:5; 1 Timothy 5:6; Hebrews 11:25

64

A Good Name

∞∞∞

A good name is more desirable than great riches;
to be esteemed is better than silver or gold.

Proverbs 22:1

Are you willing to sacrifice your good name for the gain of great riches? Is a pile of money worth diluting your influence and soiling your reputation? What price can you put on your good name? It is invaluable because it says you are not willing to sell out at any price. A noble name is a like a rare gold coin from antiquity, priceless and desirable. Like David, let your actions speak for themselves. "David behaved himself more wisely than all the servants of Saul. So his name was highly esteemed" (1 Samuel 18:30 NASB).

What is a good name? It is given by God, for God. Those with a good name make sure to give God the glory for their good deeds. Their fortress is the fear of the Lord, which keeps out unwanted influences. Those with a good name follow through with what they say. They are neither passive-aggressive nor aggressively passive, for they are forthright in both speech and motives. When you have a good name, you are willing to stand for something good and to suffer loss for what's right. You believe God blesses obedience and not manipulation for personal gain.

How do you keep your good name intact? Humility and honor are twin pillars that support a respectable reputation. For example, when you experience success, you are quick to share the limelight with the Lord and those who contributed to your good fortune. When we take credit for what we have received, we discredit our leadership. By giv-ing to others, we grow our good name.

Honor turns on the hinge of humility. Honor God and man, and your name will be honored. Respect is reciprocal. For example, will you honor a contract even when circumstances change? Are you will-ing to lose a new lease because you promised your tenant a 30-day notice? The Lord blesses landlords who keep their word and long to do the right thing. Indeed, your honor and good name depend on God.

———∞∞∞———

My salvation and my honor depend on God;
he is my mighty rock, my refuge (Psalm 62:7).

Is my goal to grow my good name or to gain wealth? Do I honor God and people in the process? How valuable is my good name?

Related Readings

1 Kings 1:47; Ecclesiasties 7:1; Luke 2:52; Acts 10:22

65

Remove Troublemakers

――――――― ∞ ―――――――

Drive out the mocker, and out goes strife;
quarrels and insults are ended.

Proverbs 22:10

Some people seem determined to set others on edge with their uncaring actions. Their goal is to get under their victims' skin and gain control. You know they are in charge when they can manipulate your emotions. They prey on good people. Chronic troublemakers listen only to what they want to hear and will not reason. They mock authority and use gossip to oppress others through fear.

Their approach may be passive or active, but the result is the same—strife, quarrels, and insults. Their influence in a situation wrecks the relationships involved. Why doesn't someone stand up to their intimidation tactics? Perhaps people are afraid of conflict or are not confident to challenge such a persuasive persona. Left alone, mockers will scoff and scorn until they get their way. They are ungracious and abusive.

So what is the leader to do? How do you respond to someone who sows discord within your organization? Ignoring them is not an option because their intensity will only increase. It's up to the leader to lead, and in this case to clearly define expectations with verbal and written communication. Perhaps another party is prodding the mocker. If so, make sure to include them in the conversation.

Make clear that if their shenanigans do not cease, they will need to transition out of the business or ministry. It is imperative you do not allow one or two people to spoil the spirit of an entire team or company.

"A little yeast works through the whole batch of dough" (Galatians 5:9). The Lord does not tolerate troublemakers.

———⚬⚬⚬———

No one who has a haughty look and an arrogant
heart will I endure (Psalm 101:5 NASB).

Will I be bold and confront pride and arrogance? Am I willing to make the hard decision for the team's sake?

Related Readings

Nehemiah 4:1-3; Proverbs 26:20-21; Matthew 18:17; 1 Corinthians 5:5-6

66

Easily Angered

Do not make friends with a hot-tempered person,
do not associate with one easily angered.

Proverbs 22:24

What's behind a short-fused temper? Why do some people fly off in rage for ridiculous reasons? Anger brings out the worst in everyone. Displays of anger are often obvious, but the root cause can be insidious. It can usually be traced to a lack of trust in God—angst in the soul. It is the expression of a faith-starved heart. Mistreatment, abandonment, rejection, and loss all contribute to anger. Anger is ugly.

It is wise to avoid the angry, lest you become like them. There is no worse feeling than being drawn into the downward spiral of someone else's fury and rage. Anger is an annoyance that no one wants to be around. It is unattractive and immature. Resentful people are so concerned for themselves, they are unable to care for others. They are caught in a cycle of self-pity and self-indulgence. But the secret to their freedom is right before their eyes—a lifestyle of serving others.

How do you avoid being drawn in by others' anger? Perhaps you start by not being intimidated by them. Do not fear the fury of the unfaithful. Moses learned this lesson. "By faith he left Egypt, not fearing the king's anger; he persevered because he saw him who is invisible" (Hebrews 11:27). Begin by faith to put these irritating individuals in God's hands. God can handle them. Don't try to change them, for they will only increase in anger. Instead, intercede to Christ on their behalf, asking that His patience and forgiveness will fill their souls. Angry hearts can be healed only by grace.

If anger controls your actions, repent and ask Jesus to set you free. A disposition of anger is not a badge of honor, but a sign of unresolved sin. Let the Lord love on you and draw you into His mercy. The Lord loves you and forgives you. He understands the proper use of anger. Ask Christ to channel your energy into eternal initiatives, such as building a church, feeding the poor, and serving your family. Be an activist for Almighty God. Passion prompted by the Holy Spirit is a mighty weapon in the hands of heaven.

—∞∞∞—

Everyone should be quick to listen, slow to speak and slow to become angry, because human anger does not produce the righteous life that God desires (James 1:19-20).

Where can I channel my energies for Christ? Whose angry outbursts and destructive behavior do I need to avoid?

Related Readings
Proverbs 29:22; Jonah 4:1-9; Ephesians 4:26-31; 1 Timothy 2:8

67

Responsible Eating

———— ∞∞ ————

When you sit to dine with a ruler; note well what is before you,
and put a knife to your throat if you are given to gluttony.
Do not crave his delicacies, for that food is deceptive.

Proverbs 23:1-3

Responsible eating is one indicator of responsible living. When we show discipline around the dinner table, we tend to exercise discipline in other areas of life. On the other hand, when we indulge our appetite, we harm our bodies. Generally, our portions should decrease as our age increases. When we eat responsibly, we can enjoy a delicious meal without gorging ourselves. We can please our palate without giving in to gluttony.

Easy access to good food can lead to cravings that spin out of control. An abundance of delicious meals makes us all overweight unless we limit our intake and exercise consistently. To enjoy a nice meal with friends and family is entertaining and relationally fulfilling, but wisdom adds temperance and moderation. An undisciplined appetite is destructive and unacceptable to the Lord.

———— ∞∞ ————

Many live as enemies of the cross of Christ.
Their destiny is destruction, their god is their
stomach, and their glory is in their shame. Their
mind is on earthly things (Philippians 3:19).

On the other hand, the fruit of the Spirit is self-control (Galatians 5:23).

How can we in good conscience eat excessively when most of the world goes to bed hungry? A careful stewardship of food will protect my body from excessive weight and will enable undernourished bodies to gain weight. How much I eat matters to my health and to the health of others. Let's not waste food while others waste away. We can eat less so others can eat more.

With this mindset, we can responsibly enjoy the blessing of delicious meals. Dine with an eye on healthy food in smaller portions. Plan menus in order to eat the right food and avoid fast food. Your body will thank you for making food your friend and not your enemy.

So whether you eat or drink or whatever you do, do
it all for the glory of God (1 Corinthians 10:31).

Do I eat responsibly? Am I careful to control my cravings for food?

Related Readings
Deuteronomy 21:20; Proverbs 25:16; 1 Corinthians 9:25-27;
2 Peter 1:6

68

A Waste of Time

Do not speak to fools,
for they will scorn your prudent words.

Proverbs 23:9

Some people do not regard wise words as worthy of attention. They may even scorn the wisdom of your words. They are intimidated by truth. Why the foolish see the truth as an enemy is dumbfounding. When others show disdain and contempt for wisdom, we need not coddle their immaturity. We need to invest our energy and attention wisely. Avoid wasting time on the foolhardy and disrespectful.

Jesus said it this way. "Don't waste what is holy on people who are unholy. Don't throw your pearls to pigs! They will trample the pearls, then turn and attack you" (Matthew 7:6 NLT). We must use discernment with our allocation of limited resources. It is better to help one grateful and genuine disciple than nine others who have no intention to change for the better. Be careful not to be deceived by hypocrites. Their goal is to bring you down to their level of cynical living.

Our Lord tenderly cares for us and protects us. He does not want us to needlessly expose ourselves to the ridicule and reproach of rascals. Do not be discouraged when people reject your wisdom. As in the parable of the soils, some hearts are not ready to receive the Word of God, so we wait for the right time.

The seed that fell among the thorns represents those who hear God's word, but all too quickly the message

is crowded out by the worries of this life and the lure
of wealth, so no fruit is produced (Matthew 13:22 NLT).

Pray for people to find the way of wisdom, but when their minds
are closed, don't waste time trying to reason with them. Let the Holy
Spirit do His work of conviction and change. Hold your relationships
with an open hand and trust the Lord to fill people's lean souls with
love. Foolish pride eventually falls, and then the wisdom of your words
will ring true and help to heal broken hearts.

―――∞∞∞―――

Blessed is the man
Who walks not in the counsel of the ungodly,
　　Nor stands in the path of sinners,
　　　Nor sits in the seat of the scornful (Psalm 1:1 NKJV).

Whom do I need to release to God and stop trying to persuade
with my own words?

Related Readings
Proverbs 9:7-8; 26:4-5; Luke 16:14-15; Acts 13:45-46

69

The Right Path

―――――∞∞∞―――――

Listen my son, and be wise,
and set your heart on the right path.

Proverbs 23:19

There is a path that leads to life and a path that leads to death. The right path does not envy sinners, but is zealous for the fear of the Lord (Proverbs 23:17). The right path does not engage in excessive drinking and eating, but is modest and responsible (verses 20-21). The right path reflects Christ and His commands. You can keep your heart on the right path by receiving and applying wisdom from God.

For example, the right path honors parents even in disagreements (verse 22). Respectful children recognize their parents' God-given authority in their lives. So they listen with longsuffering to their aging parents who repeat themselves as their minds become a bit muddled. Respectful children love their parents for who they are, not for what the children can get from them. Respectful children are motivated to listen and learn.

Those who walk on the right path reach out for direction from the Lord. They look up for His leadership, just as the psalmists did. "You have made known to me the path of life; you will fill me with joy in your presence, with eternal pleasures at your right hand" (Psalm 16:11). People on the right path experience joy and contentment as they move toward middle age. They are steady and secure as they follow their Savior's steps. "My steps have held to your paths; my feet have not stumbled" (Psalm 17:5). The right path leads to the blessing of right results.

So Providence is your Pathfinder. God is your Guide. Christ is your

Compass. Even as your path zigzags, stay focused on your faith in the Lord. The road may be rocky with unforeseen obstacles or bumpy with potholes of disappointment, but don't stray away. The right path fills your soul with gallons of God's grace. He will fuel your faith to move forward with no fear.

~~~

Our hearts had not turned back;
our feet had not strayed from your path
(Psalm 44:18).

What path is Jesus traveling? Is my heart on the right path with Him?

Related Readings

Psalm 119:32-35; Proverbs 4:10-23; Luke 3:4; Romans 11:33

70

Advisers and Guidance

∞

Surely you need guidance to wage war,
and victory is won through many advisers.

Proverbs 24:6

Acquiring godly advice takes time, but it saves you time in the long run. We are battling for our faith, our families, and our finances, so we are wise to engage wise counselors. These men and women are not perfect but have learned from their mistakes. They know how to process life with a principled paradigm. Godly guidance is a gift that keeps on giving. You pay it forward to friends and family, who benefit as well.

Who have you invited to hold you accountable? Who speaks to your spirit with words crafted in prayer, based on the Bible, and produced from a pure heart? If we are to engage the enemy effectively, we need many advisers with credible answers. As you ask for their input, listen for a theme to emerge from their counsel. This is the truth to follow. It will help you identify the dangers ahead and receive God's blessings. Wise counsel wins out.

Godly guidance gives you the grace to go far by faith. Your growth in grace allows you to understand what's best. "But grow in the grace and knowledge of our Lord and Savior Jesus Christ. To him be glory both now and forever! Amen" (2 Peter 3:18). Insight from others is the benefit you receive from their intimacy with Christ. Go to those who have been with Jesus, and you will hear from Jesus. He speaks through prayerful people.

Ask people you respect to pray that you will receive God's

perspective. "We have not stopped praying for you. We continually ask God to fill you with the knowledge of his will through all the wisdom and understanding that the Spirit gives" (Colossians 1:9). God's guidance gives you everything you need to move forward by faith. There is victory in Jesus, so engage in spiritual warfare alongside your Savior and the advisers He places in your life.

Whom can I seek out for wisdom and guidance? Am I listening with a humble heart to wise advisors?

Related Readings
Proverbs 11:14; 15:22; Luke 14:31; 1 Timothy 6:11-12

71

Lifeguard

If you say, "But we knew nothing about this,"
does not he who weighs the heart perceive it?
Does not he who guards your life know it?
Will he not repay everyone according
to what they have done?

Proverbs 24:12

The Lord guards our lives. This does not mean trouble does not frequent our comings and goings, but it does mean God is always there for us. His presence is our protector, but not to the point of precluding our free will. His guard is meant to be a reminder of righteous living and wise choices. "Let those who love the LORD hate evil, for he guards the lives of his faithful ones and delivers them from the hand of the wicked" (Psalm 97:10).

As our Lifeguard, He lets us choose where to swim—in safe waters or riskier depths. We are wise if we stay close to Him rather than floating away from His will. Wrong choices lead to unpleasant consequences. Right choices steer us toward God's blessings. Indeed, His angels are available to serve our needs, just as they served Jesus in the wilderness. "Then the devil left him, and angels came and attended him" (Matthew 4:11). Angels are waiting to attend to your body and soul.

Your life is precious to your heavenly Father. He longs for you to love Him and learn of His ways. His heart hurts when His children rebel or worry over the cares of this world. Perhaps your work has you wringing your hands. You have done everything you know to do. You have cut costs, become extremely creative, even shortened workweeks, but the future is still uncertain. In your economic instability, you can be certain that He who guards your life also guards your livelihood. Money may go, but not His provision.

As God guards your life, He empowers you to help guard others' lives. People are your greatest asset, and hard times give you the opportunity to make hard choices that validate your care for your employees. Don't give in to the fear of finances, but remain faithful to do what's right, and God will provide in His good time. Leaders learn more about leadership in lean times than in times of plenty. During difficult days, put into practice the values you discussed during the days of abundance. The Lord is your Lifeguard. Follow His example as you care for others.

———∞∞∞———

Are not all angels ministering spirits sent to serve
those who will inherit salvation? (Hebrews 1:14).

Am I at peace with the Lord's protection? Do those in my care know I have their backs?

Related Readings
Psalm 44:21; Proverbs 5:21; Luke 4:10; Philippians 4:7

72

Keep Showing Up

*For though the righteous fall seven times, they rise again,
but the wicked stumble when calamity strikes.*

Proverbs 24:16

Do you ever struggle with stamina? Do you sometimes need extra motivation to keep showing up at work, to continue being truly present in relationships, and to maintain your commitment to serve? Do you ask yourself, "Is it really worth it? Will things ever change?" I struggle with this and sometimes wonder if I am in God's will. I occasionally pause and ponder the thought of moving on from the mess in front of me. But if Christ has called me to this mission, I am compelled to complete the task. I show up because this is my Savior's expectation.

We keep showing up and remain faithful because our heavenly Father never promised that this life would be without problems and challenges. "A righteous person may have many troubles, but the LORD delivers him from them all" (Psalm 34:19). The cares of this world will try to choke His Word out of our hearts, but we can withstand the pressure through prayer. This is our relief valve that vents frustrations. Our Father in heaven understands. Don't lie in self-pity, but reach out to the Lord and let Him lift you up.

We will fall down and scrape our soul, bruise our pride, and arouse our anger. However, a disciple of Christ is determined to remain faithful. Keep showing up when others let you down. Keep showing up when your finances fade. Keep showing up when you are treated unfairly. Keep showing up when you are sad and uncertain. Keep showing up, and God's grace will break in and fill you with peace. He blesses righteous resilience.

Rise from your fall into sin and face your Savior with remorse and repentance. Rise from your fall under the sin of others and face your enemies with forgiveness and grace. Rise from your financial free fall and face life with faith and generosity. Jesus showed up for you on the old rugged cross amid the world's injustice and His own brokenness. He still shows up, ever interceding on your behalf.

Who will bring any charge against those whom
God has chosen? It is God who justifies. Who then
is the one who condemns? Christ Jesus who died—
more than that, who was raised to life—is at the
right hand of God and is also interceding for us.
Who shall separate us from the love of Christ? Shall
trouble or hardship or persecution or famine or
nakedness or danger or sword? (Romans 8:33-35).

Do I regularly thank the Lord for showing up for me? Will I show up on behalf of others?

Related Readings
Psalm 37:24; Micah 7:8-10; Matthew 18:21-22; 2 Corinthians 1:8-10

73

The Refining Process

———— ∞ ————

Remove the dross from the silver,
and a silversmith can produce a vessel.

Proverbs 25:4

We are all in a refining process. The Bible calls this sanctification. Our most difficult days are meant to make us more like Jesus. God does not waste pain. Rather, He uses it for our purification. "For you, God, tested us; you refined us like silver" (Psalm 66:10). Enduring the refining process is not easy, but it is essential if we are to cultivate an eternal perspective. We need the fires of suffering to extract the dross hidden in our fleshly habits.

Dross is anything that is dirty and of little or no value. It is waste or impure matter, the scum that rises to the surface of molten metal. The pressure you may feel in your life is pushing impurities to the surface of your soul. This allows God's Spirit to skim off the sin so you are free and clean in Christ. Don't resist the righteous refining process. It is the Lord's way to make you holy for Him. Refinement is a requisite for righteousness.

Even the wise and most capable for Christ are subject to the Almighty's refining fires. "Some of the wise will stumble, so that they may be refined, purified and made spotless until the time of the end, for it will still come at the appointed time" (Daniel 11:35). The affliction you endure will refine your leadership skills so you can lead your team to the next level. Your example of faithfulness under fire will inspire your followers.

Your refinement is an expression of the Lord's love. He loves you too much to allow you to be held back by immature attitudes and impure motives. Because He cares, He continues to remove layers of hurt that need healing and sin that needs forgiving. Submit to His sanctifying process, and your purification will propel you forward in His perfect will.

For this is the will of God, your sanctification: that you should abstain from sexual immorality; that each of you should know how to possess his own vessel in sanctification and honor (1 Thessalonians 4:3-4 NKJV).

Am I surrendered to my Savior's process of refinement? Do I daily confess my sin and receive His cleansing power for my soul?

Related Readings
Isaiah 48:10; Daniel 12:10; 2 Timothy 2:20-21; 1 Peter 1:7

74

A Cooldown Period

What you have seen with your eyes
do not bring hastily to court,
for what will you do in the end
if your neighbor puts you to shame?

Proverbs 25:7-8

B e careful not to react too quickly. Words spoken in the heat of hurt or the rage of anger can come back to haunt you, especially if your rash actions lead to a lawsuit. If you commit to legal action without weighing the emotional and financial cost, you may very well regret you went down this long and lonely road, even if you win. Consider the expense before you pursue legal action. Cool down and then decide.

Perhaps you need a break to reflect on your options and seek godly counsel. A striving soul only becomes more entangled in emotional upheaval. You need to unwind your vexed will and receive solace from your Savior Jesus. This was David's approach under pressure. "I called to the LORD, who is worthy of praise, and have been saved from my enemies" (2 Samuel 22:4). Cool down so you can see Christ's faithfulness.

There are ways to settle disputes in private. You may need a mediator to manage the communication with your antagonist. If both parties have overdrawn their relational equity, they both feel they deserve a debt of compliance. Communication takes place best when it is calm and quiet. "A gentle answer turns away wrath, but a harsh word stirs up anger" (Proverbs 15:1). Model the way by managing your emotions.

So go away with Christ and cool down before you act. Make reconciliation your goal, not revenge. Remember that you are a minister of reconciliation. Once you cool down, ask what Christ would have you do. A cool head leads to a warm heart. There is no shame in seeking to make things right and reconnecting in Christ.

———∞∞∞———

All this is from God, who reconciled us to
himself through Christ and gave us the ministry
of reconciliation (2 Corinthians 5:18).

Have I been wishing for revenge in any situation? What steps can I take to make amends and facilitate reconciliation—even where I am innocent?

Related Readings

Judges 11:12; Proverbs 20:3; Luke 14:31-32; 1 Corinthians 6:1

75

Refreshing Relationships

—∞∞∞—

Like a snow-cooled drink at harvest time
is a trustworthy messenger to the one who sends him;
he refreshes the spirit of his master.

Proverbs 25:13

Some people energize and encourage everyone they meet. Their servant spirit empowers the people in their path. Because they are trustworthy, no one doubts that they will do what they say in a timely and thorough manner. These refreshing people use encouragement to make sad spirits rise in hope and anticipation. Make sure you honor those who refresh you. Give them your gratitude and pray for them to continue.

—∞∞∞—

They refreshed my spirit and yours also. Such
men deserve recognition (1 Corinthians 16:18).

Where do they get this ability to refresh others? How are they able to not exhaust its reserves? The Lord refreshes refreshing people. "Six days do your work, but on the seventh day do not work, so that your ox and your donkey may rest, and so that the slave born in your household and the foreigner living among you may be refreshed" (Exodus 23:12). If work is your life, you have nothing left over to give. Learn to let the Lord regularly refresh your exhausted emotions.

Do you have a regular routine of receiving refreshment from heaven? You might walk during your lunch break, listen to soothing music in the evening, or read your Bible in the morning. Hike a mountain or swim in the sea...somehow, engage in the beauty of God's creation, and you will be refreshed. Christ's refreshment is waiting for those who are weary and worn out. "I will refresh the weary and satisfy the faint" (Jeremiah 31:25). Like a refreshing cold drink on a blistering hot day, the Lord's love quenches thirsty hearts.

You feel the most spiritual after the Lord has refreshed your mind, body, soul, and spirit. Therefore, make sure that you are refreshed so you can refresh others. The Christian community is called to refresh those in the wake of its influence. Refreshment is reciprocal, so receive it freely and give it freely for Christ's sake.

———∞———

In addition to our own encouragement,
we were especially delighted to see how
happy Titus was, because his spirit has been
refreshed by all of you (2 Corinthians 7:14).

Whom can I refresh with a kind word or comforting Scripture? Whom do I know whose shriveled soul needs an infusion of hope and love?

Related Readings
Genesis 18:5; Proverbs 11:25; Romans 15:31-33; Philemon 1:20

76

Diligence, Not Excuses

*A sluggard says, "There's a lion in the road,
a fierce lion roaming the streets!"*

Proverbs 26:13

Excuses are the language of the lazy. Instead of taking responsibility, they assign blame. The project hasn't been completed because of what someone else hasn't done. The weather disrupted a deadline, a vendor delayed, an illness struck a team member, traffic made me late, we need more resources, "they" changed their mind, the company doesn't communicate, I am overwhelmed and I need more time… Where diligence is not in play, any excuse will do. In Solomon's day, would-be workers feared wild animals. Today we are more likely to fear our own failure.

We overcome our excuses by diligently focusing on our priorities.

Diligence is encouraged by what can be done, not discouraged by what can't be done. Instead of procrastinating, the diligent are proactive. They are motivated by potential outcomes that will make them and those around them better. For example, diligent people don't talk about reading a book one day. They set up a simple process of reading (or listening to) a chapter a day. After 30 days, they have completed a 30-chapter book or two books with 15 chapters. The motto of the diligent is, "No excuses, only ways to move forward." Let resourcefulness brighten your horizons.

꧁꧂

> Go to the ant, you sluggard;
>> consider its ways and be wise!
> It has no commander,
>> no overseer or ruler,
> yet it stores its provisions in summer
>> and gathers its food at harvest (Proverbs 6:6-8).

Like the teeny, tiny, insignificant ant, we learn to prepare. We don't wait until a week before company comes to visit our home before we plan for their comfort. We ask ourselves what needs to be done—closets de-cluttered, bathrooms cleaned, menus made, and groceries bought. Not surprisingly, the blessing of hosting guests motivates us to do what we've discussed doing for months. The diligent look for reasons to do what's important.

Most importantly, we are diligent to grow our faith in God. No excuses, only creative ways to facilitate more of Christ in our character. We plan for intimate encounters with Jesus. We calendar solitude to quiet our soul so we can hear the Lord. An innovative mind comes alive when it's fed a steady diet of margin. Our diligence to become loving disciples of Jesus Christ benefits our whole being. So we seek our Savior, and He meets us on His terms. In humility we receive His grace for living. Diligence finds rest from self-reliance by trusting Jesus.

꧁꧂

Diligently obey the Lord your God (Zechariah 6:15).

Heavenly Father, keep me diligently focused on Your priorities and deliver me from making excuses—especially lame ones.

Related Readings

Proverbs 10:4; 12:24-27; Ecclesiastes 11:4; Romans 12:8; 1 Timothy 4:15

77

Discretion, Not Gossip

Without wood a fire goes out;
without gossip a quarrel dies down.

Proverbs 26:20

Gossip is the go-to behavior for those who want to get back at someone. Maybe they were hurt and this is their passive way to inflict pain. Or, motivated by insecurity, they feel the need to build themselves up by putting others down. This idle talk or rumor only exposes the immature heart of the instigator. Misinformation by the misinformed leads to confusion at the least and clouds character at the worse.

Thus, by God's grace we refrain from fueling the fires of gossip. A discreet heart pauses before it is tempted to tickle people's ears. It maintains a noble commitment to facilitate conversation around ideas, not default to lazy discussions that demean people. Discretion protects our souls from embarrassing entanglements that later prove to be lies or half-truths. For example, we may talk about someone's long lunches at work, not knowing they visit their elderly parent in a nursing home. Discretion is a diligent fact finder and is slow to find fault.

Discretion will protect you,
and understanding will guard you (Proverbs 2:11).

How can we practice discretion when other people begin to gossip? First of all, we recognize gossip as a deterrent to a healthy culture at home and work. It creates factions, contributes to mistrust and disloyalty, and erodes productivity. When we politely dismiss discussions based on hearsay, we imply to the gossiper, "You do not have control over me or the person you are dishonoring." Instead of keeping quiet we say in love, "I'm surprised—I've always known her to be a hard worker."

Above all else, we seek our heavenly Father for wisdom and discretion. Discretion is embedded in a heart of wisdom. Without discretion we are not wise, but foolish. Yes, a commitment not to offend others and to respect their privacy is the fruit of wisdom and grace. We become trusted confidants when our trust is in Christ. Gossip is an unused, unintelligible, foreign language to a faithful follower of Jesus. Our discretion provides a safe environment for needy souls.

> I wisdom, dwell together with prudence;
> I possess knowledge and discretion.
> To fear the LORD is to hate evil;
> I hate pride and arrogance,
> evil behavior and perverse speech
> (Proverbs 8:12-13).

Heavenly Father, give me a discreet heart that honors You and others.

Related Readings
1 Chronicles 22:12; Proverbs 11:12-13; 16:28; Romans 1:28-32; 2 Thessalonians 3:11

78

Deception Self-Destructs

∞

Whoever digs a pit will fall into it;
if someone rolls a stone, it will roll back on them.

Proverbs 26:27

Deception is the preferred behavior of those who delight in presenting a false persona. They have an unhealthy determination to outdo others, impress the crowd, and draw attention to their alleged accomplishments. Their words are charming to your face, but behind your back their conversations are caustic. Insecure people are compelled to seek security in deceptive behavior. They are masters at presenting a mirage.

Devising sly schemes requires a breathtaking amount of energy. When a man or woman's heart is changed by Christ, that same amount of effort can be exerted toward eternal matters. Jesus jump-starts a soul on the journey out of self-deception and into faith. Otherwise, deceivers' destiny may be like Haman's, who hung on the gallows of his own making. "So they impaled Haman on the pole he had set up for Mordecai. Then the king's fury subsided" (Esther 7:10). Deception can be deadly.

So how do you handle people who are intent on conniving and deceiving? Maybe a bully is using her position to promote herself to the demise of her team members. Perhaps an adult child maliciously seeks to cut his siblings out of their parents' will. Or maybe your business partner, whom you thought walked in integrity, was caught stealing.

First, make sure you are free from any of your own self-imposed deception. Come clean with Christ and others.

161

Second, Christlike confrontation is necessary to expose a deceiver's agenda. Go to them with gentleness and humility with the goal of restoration. "Brothers and sisters, if someone is caught in a sin, you who live by the Spirit should restore that person gently. But watch yourselves, or you also may be tempted" (Galatians 6:1). If there is still no remorse, deception carries a consequence of its own.

Am I aware of my own devious tendencies? Have I repented of my own failures? Am I willing to confront someone else whose behavior is deceptive and destructive?

Related Readings
Psalms 7:15-16; 9:15-16; 2 Corinthians 4:2; Galatians 6:7

79

Focus on Today

Do not boast about tomorrow,
for you do not know what a day may bring.

Proverbs 27:1

Today is the only time we have for certain, so we ask, "What can I do today to further God's plan for my life, both professionally and personally?" Consider praying a similar prayer each day to recalibrate your understanding of what Christ wants for you. This is how Jesus taught us to pray: "When you pray, say: 'Father, hallowed be your name, your kingdom come. Give us each day our daily bread'" (Luke 11:2-3). Daily bread is God's reminder of our desperate need for Him.

If we only dream about tomorrow, today's responsibilities lose their attraction, and we can become irresponsible. Future ambition must not undermine our attention to current commitments. Today you can trust the Lord. You can love family and friends. Today you can serve a stranger, meet a deadline at work, babysit for a neighbor, go to the doctor, or plan your next special time with your spouse. Focus on today, and you'll find fulfillment. Obsess about tomorrow, and you'll become sick with discontentment.

Presuming on tomorrow can put us into a predicament. This is why debt is deceptive and dangerous. Aggressive borrowing can bring down our financial house. We cannot expect to expand our business on the uncertainty of credit. We cannot promise ourselves ease of life and entitlement to affluence. Christ is our provider. "If it is the Lord's will, we will live and do this or that" (James 4:15). Faith is our filter for future opportunities.

God's activity is not easily discerned. By design He invites dependence. Therefore focus on today by faith and feel the assurance of His activity on your behalf.

Just as you do not know the path of the wind and
how bones are formed in the womb of the pregnant
woman, so you do not know the activity of God
who makes all things (Ecclesiastes 11:5 NASB).

What current commitment needs my undivided attention? Do I need to replace any future presumptions with present prayer and planning?

Related Readings
Ecclesiastes 3:22; Isaiah 56:12; Matthew 6:34; James 4:13-15

80

Faithful Friendship

◊◊◊

Perfume and incense bring joy to the heart,
and the pleasantness of a friend
springs from their heartfelt advice.
Do not forsake your friend or a friend of your family.

Proverbs 27:9-10

A faithful friendship is a relational fortress that protects you from hurt feelings and misunderstandings. When you decide beforehand to forgive and forget, there is no room for lingering resentment. Faithful friendship rises above petty arguments and selfish actions. True friends determine to push through relational obstacles peacefully through prayer and patience. As Jonathan said to David, "Go in peace, for we have sworn friendship with each other in the name of the LORD" (1 Samuel 20:42).

Christian friendships are based on the character of Christ. Each person attempts to out-serve the other because Jesus prioritized serving others. Best friends forever look for ways to love without fanfare, and they get more excited about giving than receiving. They celebrate this transaction of double blessing. Jesus said, "It is more blessed to give than receive" (Acts 20:35). Faithful friends bring joy to each other's heart.

It is good to have friends close by. You enjoy their company because it provides a safe and secure place for you to be yourself. You can laugh heartily and cry unashamedly. Do you have a close confidant who gives you earnest counsel? Do you have a trusted advisor full of wisdom and discernment? Look to friends of the family who have a track record of faithfulness and wise advice. You honor your parents when you honor their friends.

Faithful friendships are a reflection of your relationship with the Lord. They are permanent and full of grace and truth.

———∞∞∞———

After Job had prayed for his friends, the LORD
restored his fortunes and gave him twice
as much as he had before (Job 42:10).

Is there a faithful friendship I need to rekindle by reaching out with a phone call or visit? Whom do I need to thank for their faithful friendship all these years?

Related Readings

Ezra 10:2-5; Song of Songs 4:10; Acts 28:15; 2 Corinthians 2:15-16

81

The Test of Praise

꩜

The crucible for silver and the furnace for gold,
but people are tested by their praise.

Proverbs 27:21

The test of praise reveals whether our motives are pure. Why do I do what I do? If it is for the praise of men, then I have misdirected motives. My faith has faltered because I am more concerned about pleasing people than pleasing my Master Jesus. "How can you believe since you accept glory from one another but do not seek the glory that comes from the only God?" (John 5:44). Praise from God builds belief and activates obedience.

Jesus did not receive man's praise. "I do not accept glory from human beings" (verse 41). He knew the danger of being enamored by earthly accolades instead of humbled by heaven's honor. When the Lord leads you into a mission that the masses don't understand, don't be swayed. Stay the course with Christ because all that really matters are the words He will one day say to you—"Well done." Listen for the applause of heaven and let it drown out any ovations on earth.

The test of praise makes you more thankful and less critical, more respectful and less condescending, more patient and less demanding, and more diligent to learn and less inclined to grow lazy. When praise and glory come your way, make sure you reflect it toward your heavenly Father. Proud Herod forgot this. "Immediately, because Herod did not give praise to God, an angel of the Lord struck him down, and he was eaten by worms and died" (Acts 12:23). Anything praiseworthy in life comes to us as a result of God's blessings.

So when sincere saints offer you compliments, quietly give them up to Christ. A courteous thank you and a private prayer of thanksgiving to God go a long way to passing the test of praise. Before long, people will begin praising the Lord because of your service.

———∞∞∞———

Because of the service by which you have
proved yourselves, others will praise God for the
obedience that accompanies your confession
of the gospel of Christ (2 Corinthians 9:13).

Do I let go of praise and leave it with the Lord? Do I praise God for His grace?

Related Readings
2 Chronicles 20:21; Psalm 56:4; John 12:43; 1 Thessalonians 2:6

82

Stand Your Ground

The wicked flee though no one pursues,
but the righteous are as bold as a lion.

Proverbs 28:1

Boldness comes from being with Christ. He empowers the righteous to do the right things the right way. Your intimacy with the Almighty empowers you to engage the enemy and endure hardships. Indeed, the fruit of great challenge is great reward. So stand your ground for God and do not give in to fear and doubt. If you rely on yourself you will fail, but if you rely on the Lord you will succeed.

Self-reliance crumbles when circumstances become grim. People without God as their guide run away in fear, but the righteous take heart and hold on to heaven's inheritance. They are bold and remain strong because they see their Savior Jesus as the initiator and completer of the cause. As you remain poised in prayer to God, take the time to share with others what you receive from Him. Develop your leaders and give others the resources they need to succeed.

Followers need a leader who is not caught up in self-preservation, but captivated by Christ. A bold leader is not preoccupied with an exit strategy. Rather, he or she is focused on processing problems with creative solutions. A culture of confidence takes root when everyone is committed to thriving in excellence and not just surviving in mediocrity. Fear senses the possibility of failure behind every challenge, but faith sees opportunity rise out of anguish.

Therefore, stand your ground with God. The enemy has no authority over you—especially your emotions. His is a phantom pursuit. Stay rooted in righteous acts with a hopeful attitude, and Almighty God will bless your efforts. You are bold when you have been with Jesus.

> When they saw the courage of Peter and John
> and realized that they were unschooled, ordinary
> men, they were astonished and they took note
> that these men had been with Jesus (Acts 4:13).

Is my security in myself or in my Savior Jesus Christ?

Related Readings

2 Kings 7:6-7; Psalm 53:5; Acts 14:3; 1 Thessalonians 2:2

Discerning People Obey God

∞

A discerning son heeds instruction,
but a companion of gluttons disgraces his father.

Proverbs 28:7

Discernment is the ability to see things as they are and determine what God expects. Discerning college students resist following the crowd into embarrassing situations. Discerning leaders understand the urgent need of a situation and call for action. Discerning nations comprehend the dire consequences of abandoning common sense and shutting out the Lord.

∞

They are a nation without sense,
   there is no discernment in them.
If only they were wise and would understand this
   and discern what their end will be!
      (Deuteronomy 32:28-29).

We need discernment to protect us from ourselves and others. For example, your family may be weighing a financial decision. Your spouse is hesitant because of the risk, and you are confident of a best-case scenario. What is the downside of waiting and taking a more conservative approach to managing cash? The check in his or her spirit may be the Lord's protection. Invite advice, and you will become wiser.

———∞∞∞———

A rebuke impresses a discerning person
more than a hundred lashes a fool (Proverbs 17:10).

Remember, there are educated fools and self-educated sages. A wealthy person may be smart in the world and ignorant of the Lord, while a poor person may be ignorant by the world's standards but perceptive in God's ways. "The rich are wise in their own eyes; one who is poor and discerning sees how deluded they are" (Proverbs 28:11). Do not discriminate against discerning voices from unlikely places. Strangers, enemies, and subordinates may all help you clarify the wise thing to do.

So seek to discern God's way and obey. Your discernment may open doors of incredible influence, just as Joseph's did. "Pharaoh said to Joseph, 'Since God has made all this known to you, there is no one so discerning and wise as you'" (Genesis 41:39). Discernment is a gift from God for God. It is a directive from the Spirit of God.

———∞∞∞———

The person without the Spirit does not accept
the things that come from the Spirit of God
but considers them foolishness, and cannot
understand them because they are discerned
only through the Spirit (1 Corinthians 2:14).

Do I prayerfully discern God's best and then obey?

Related Readings

Psalm 119:125; Hosea 14:9; Romans 12:16; Philippians 1:9-10

84

An Opportunity to Change

*Whoever remains stiff-necked after many rebukes
will suddenly be destroyed—without remedy.*

Proverbs 29:1

God gives us opportunities to change—not for change's sake, but for Christ's sake. The change that seems to challenge us the most is the conversion of wrong thinking into right thinking. Why is this so? What causes us at times to resist righteous and loving rebukes from friends and family? We first have to look at our hearts and make sure humility is at home and not pride. Stubborn pride flees in the face of a humble heart that listens.

It's tempting to just amend our current dysfunctional actions and ignore the need for an internal transformation of thinking. However, a mind captured by Christ invites others to challenge its categories. "We take captive every thought to make it obedient to Christ" (2 Corinthians 10:5). Those who have been touched deeply by the grace of God gain a humble and teachable spirit. Openness to instruction is an opportunity for growth.

Rebuke the discerning, and they will
gain knowledge (Proverbs 19:25).

When things don't go your way, look for a better way. Perhaps by letting go of short-term control, you will gain much more long-term influence. But if you buck the process of accountability, you could suffer the loss of valuable relationships and your respected reputation in the community. There is no righteous remedy for those stuck in an obstinate attitude, unwilling to listen to authority's voice. Destruction awaits determined dysfunctional behavior, bringing a sad conclusion to what may have been a sincere start.

Fortunately, grace gives multiple opportunities to listen to the voice of reason. We can invite change at any moment and learn how to be loved by receiving caring correction and wise rebukes.

—⚭—

Repent at my rebuke!
Then I will pour out my thoughts to you,
I will make known to you my teachings
(Proverbs 1:23).

What areas of my life need to change? Do I wisely receive loving rebukes from the Lord and from loved ones in my life?

Related Readings

Psalm 39:11; Proverbs 9:8; Luke 17:3; 1 Timothy 5:1

85

Compelling Vision

———— ∞ ————

Where there is no vision, the people perish:
but he that keepeth the law, happy is he.

Proverbs 29:18 KJV

How God-sized is your vision? Is it doomed to failure unless your heavenly Father comes through? Hard times can challenge your dreams and chip away at your passionate confidence that the Lord will deliver large results. But His vision brought you to this place, and His vision will propel you forward. Rise above any earthly excuses and, like Nehemiah, be bold to ask for provisions from unconventional sources. "It pleased the king to send me; so I set a time" (Nehemiah 2:6).

Our King of kings, Jesus Christ, is waiting to work through earthly authorities on our behalf. Our part is to prayerfully show up with a plan and ask unashamedly with a compelling vision. Don't waste time wondering if it is the right time. Set a time and trust the Lord to come through beyond your expectations. Collaborate with Christ. Get counsel from godly advisors and then present your case by faith.

You have worked hard, overcome adversity, and sacrificed to see your dream come true. Big visions attract big people and big resources. Without a compelling vision, your resources and relationships will continue to dwindle, but with a compelling vision, they will flourish. A big vision of the Lord brings out the best in you and in others. Keep Christ the central focus of your faith and be faithful to His compelling call.

Ask yourself, "Do I confidently cast a compelling vision? Am I trusting the Lord for big things, or am I bound up by earthly expectations?"

A compelling vision is your motivation to move forward by faith and see your heavenly Father work in ways you can't imagine.

For this reason I bow my knees to the Father...that you, being rooted and grounded in love, may be able...to know the love of Christ which passes knowledge, that you may be filled with all the fullness of God. Now to Him who is able to do exceeding abundantly above all that we ask or think, according to the power that works in us, to Him be glory in the church by Christ Jesus to all generations, forever and ever. Amen (Ephesians 3:14-21 NKJV).

Is my vision aligned with the Lord's vision for my life and work?

Related Readings
Genesis 15:1; Daniel 1:17; Luke 19:41-42; Acts 9:10-13

86

Daily Bread

―――――― ᴄᴀᴏ ――――――

Keep falsehood and lies far from me;
give me neither poverty nor riches,
but give me only my daily bread.

Proverbs 30:8

Why is it necessary for the follower of Jesus Christ to focus his faith on daily bread? One compelling reason is that it defines our dependence on Him. It is the intuitive need to keep our soul empty of sin's enticements (lies, laziness, and greed) and our body full of food (daily bread). Jesus taught His disciples to pray, "Give us today our daily bread...And lead us not into temptation, but deliver us from the evil one" (Matthew 6:11,13).

Can we really make it through life successfully without the Lord's loving leadership, compassionate comfort, and wise rebuke? Of course not! A life untethered from holy reliance is aimless and interested only in fulfilling fleshy desires the world's way. In contrast, men and women with an appetite for the Almighty "hunger and thirst for righteousness" (Matthew 5:5). They have an innate passion—born at regeneration—to engage every day with the Provider in a prayerful posture of dependence.

Your dispenser of daily bread is totally trustworthy and has a proven track record of giving to His children everything they need. Are you content with Christ's daily provisions? Or do you still struggle with wanting to prescribe to Providence your wants and wishes? Peace comes when we receive His prescriptions for living and leave the unknowns in His hands. His part is to give daily bread, and our part is to gratefully receive it.

When you live in between affliction and riches, you are in an authentic position to serve others. Most people can relate to your life when you are transparent about your own struggles and fears as well as your successes. Leverage your dependence on the Lord as a model to lead others to love Him more than their own lives. Daily bread is an opportunity to engage others.

Your need for His daily bread deepens your faith and broadens your influence. Therefore, wake up each day grateful for God's goodness and the glory of His provisions. His provision of daily bread deepens your dependence on Him.

———∞∞∞———

I have not departed from the commands of his lips;
I have treasured the words of his mouth
more than my daily bread (Job 23:12).

Am I satisfied with the daily bread God provides? Do I feed off of faith in Jesus and faithful living?

Related Readings
Genesis 28:20; Psalm 119:29-37; Luke 11:3; 1 Timothy 6:6-8

87

The Question of Affluence

―――――∞∞――――――

*Otherwise I may have too much and disown you
and say, "Who is the Lord?"*

Proverbs 30:9

How much is enough? Asking this question helps us to keep the love of money from dissolving our faith. The pursuit of cash, left unchecked, tends to leave the Lord out of our conversations. Unless we ask ourselves this wise question, we will eventually ask a foolish one—"Who is the Lord?" An unchecked desire for affluence will eventually weaken your devotion to Christ.

Jesus made this clear when He addressed those who loved riches. "'You cannot serve both God and Money.' The Pharisees, who loved money, heard all this and were sneering at Jesus" (Luke 16:13-14). Focusing on our net worth can be a temptation for everyone—young and old, religious and secular, Westerners and Easterners...we all can become entangled by earthly riches. Honestly ask yourself, "Has Christ or cash captured the affections of my heart?"

Prosperity can make us proud and lead us to dismiss the Lord, or at least to seek Him only during difficult situations in our lives, such as sickness, death, divorce, and job loss. If we feel no need for faith in God, we will not feel obligated to obey Him. However, heaven is pleased when you consider prosperity less important than the will of God. He will help you loosen your grip on stuff until, with an open hand, you give back to Him what was already His.

Generosity governs your devotion to God. As you humbly handle earthly wealth well, you will experience the true riches of intimacy with Jesus and the satisfaction of serving Him alone. Freedom from money is freedom to love God and people. He is the owner of our lives and our stuff.

—∞∞∞—

So if you have not been trustworthy in handling worldly wealth, who will trust you with true riches? (Luke 16:11).

How much is enough for my family? Are we free to serve Christ and others, or are we distracted by our desire for wealth? Who is the Lord of my family?

Related Readings

Psalm 10:4; Ezekiel 13:3; Luke 6:46; 1 Timothy 6:10

88

Sober Leadership

∞

It is not for kings, Lemuel—
it is not for kings to drink wine, not for rulers to crave beer,
lest they drink and forget what has been decreed,
and deprive all the oppressed of their rights.

Proverbs 31:4-5

Sobriety is required for serious leaders. Men and women who seek what's best for the team cannot be compromised by inebriation. Alcohol and drugs can cause people in power to pretend one thing and do another. In casual settings, leaders must not compromise their integrity by engaging in overly familiar behavior.

The apostle Paul provides this description of leaders in the church: "Deacons are to be worthy of respect, sincere, not indulging in much wine, and not pursuing dishonest gain. They must keep hold of the deep truths of the faith with a clear conscience" (1 Timothy 3:8-9). Sober leadership sets an example for other team members to follow. What the leader tolerates in moderation, the less mature may take to the extreme.

What guidelines protect your own decision making? What behavior do you decide on before attending a company party or a business trip where your associates expect to participate in shady social activities? You can easily get lured into a regrettable situation if you don't set behavioral boundaries. Consider focusing on work during the workweek and enjoying rest and relaxation with friends and family on the weekend. Mixing business and pleasure can be unproductive and even destructive.

Sober leadership sends a message of sincerity and a sense of urgency. It is not void of joy and laughter, but there is an undertone of discipline and seriousness that invites loyalty. Stay sober as a leader, and you will reap the rewards of respect and results. Ask others to confront your questionable decisions and actions. Fools muddle their way through confused thinking, but sober-minded leaders are clearheaded and humble before God.

Do not think of yourself more highly than
you ought, but rather think of yourself
with sober judgment (Romans 12:3).

Is my leadership sober minded? Am I conscious of Christ's wisdom?

Related Readings

Exodus 18:25; 1 Samuel 25:26-28; Hebrews 13:7; 1 Timothy 3:1-7

89

Speak Up

*Speak up for those who cannot speak for themselves,
for the rights of all who are destitute.
Speak up and judge fairly;
defend the rights of the poor and needy.*

Proverbs 31:8-9

Some people cannot speak up for themselves. The widow and orphan who are in distress desperately need compassionate and competent advocates. Children trapped in human trafficking need to be rescued by the righteous. The unborn cry out for a merciful voice. Foster children who are emotionally spent pray for families to speak up and invite them into their homes. The poor and needy need legal, economic, and spiritual advocacy to advance their cause. All around us, groups and individuals are stuck for lack of one person who will boldly speak up.

We who are saved are called by our Savior to say something or do something. If we won't, who will? How can we remain unmoved while one child remains exploited, one family is hungry, one orphan is homeless, or one widow is destitute? We have an obligation to speak up for those whose rights have been ignored. Social systems are limited and rarely include a spiritual component. But those of us who have been rescued by the grace and love of our Lord God are rich in His resources. We must speak up!

Jonathan spoke well of David to Saul his father and
said to him, "Let not the king do wrong to his servant

David; he has not wronged you, and what he has
done has benefited you greatly" (1 Samuel 19:4).

Almost every day we have opportunities to speak up for someone or to leave them alone and vulnerable. Whom can we defend at work? An associate who may have lost favor with a peer or supervisor? When people speak poorly of a friend or family member, we can point out the person's good traits and give them the benefit of the doubt. Silence is not an option for a courageous and caring heart. Love has the back of those who don't know what they don't know. Love can't keep quiet!

Above all, where do we need to speak up for our Savior's sake? He does not need defending, but we need to be clear where we stand with Christ. We speak up for what breaks His heart. We are on a mission to fight injustice. We serve sinners for whom Jesus died. We speak up for the lost in prayer, so they too might come to celebrate the saving grace of God. Jesus speaks up today and says, "I forgive you," so we do too. He says, "I love you," so we echo His words. What our Master says to say and do, we say and do!

Remember that I stood before you
and spoke in their behalf
to turn your wrath away from them (Jeremiah 18:20).

Heavenly Father, break my heart for what breaks Yours. Give me courage to speak up.

Related Readings
Genesis 50:4; 1 Kings 2:19; Ezekiel 3:17; John 12:49;
Ephesians 4:25; 6:19

90

The Virtuous Woman

꩜

A wife of noble character who can find?
She is worth far more than rubies.

Proverbs 31:10

A woman of character is not easily found. She is rare and valuable. Because of her appealing attributes, she is a gift from God. Thank Him often if you are blessed with a woman like this in your life. She is rare because she focuses on others even in our self-crazed culture. For the follower of Christ, selflessness is expected. But for our society as a whole, it is an anomaly. The noble woman refuses to lower herself to a standard of mediocrity.

Her goal is excellence in living. Duplicity is not an option for her. Rather, she serves with authenticity and industry. No skills or gifts remain dormant in her active life. She channels her energies into the welfare of her family and is resourceful with financial opportunities. A noble woman is an anchor for her family. Her character provides stability when challenges creep into her home. She is determined to do the right thing regardless of the difficulties it may require. Character is more important than compromise, so she models the way for her friends and family. She is a rock of hope for others because God's Word has become that for her.

However, be careful to not take the world on your shoulders—that is God's job. Also, do not hold yourself to a standard of perfection. Leave yourself some wiggle room for mistakes. You will make mistakes. Let mistakes teach you what to do and what not to do in the future. They are reminders of your dependence on God. Your goal is not to live a mistake-free life, but to love God and love people. Let Him continue to develop your character and grow you into a mentor of other women. Don't waste your wonderful experiences. Share them with younger women so they can grow in their character.

Husband, love your wife of character. Tell her often how proud you are of her. Don't be intimidated by her level of spirituality. On the contrary, celebrate her passion for life and her spiritual maturity. Allow her life to challenge you and inspire you to the same level of character development.

Her influence is ever-present in her work and home. Encourage her burgeoning influence and opportunities. Become her biggest cheerleader. If she wants to start a business, help her start a business. If she needs some help with the house and lawn, make that investment. Free her to do what she does best.

Allow her to reach her full potential. Give her the cash, confidence, and resources to reach for her dreams. Be grateful. A woman of character is not to be taken for granted. Help her to pace herself, and protect her from the encroachment of those with warped motives. Her character is a valued asset that needs to be managed with care. Care for her as she cares for you!

In the same way you married men should live considerately with [your wives], with an intelligent recognition [of the marriage relation], honoring the woman as [physically] the weaker, but [realizing that you] are joint heirs of the grace (God's unmerited favor) of life, in order that your prayers may not be hindered and cut off. [Otherwise you cannot pray effectively] (1 Peter 3:7 AMP).

Heavenly Father, use my submitted life to You as a blessing to those who You bring into my life.

Related Readings
Job 33:26; Proverbs 12:4; 14:1; Ruth 3:11; Colossians 3:13-15

How to Become a
Disciple of Jesus Christ

⸻

Holy Scripture teaches us how to become disciples and how to make disciples.

> Then Jesus came to them and said, "All authority in heaven and on earth has been given to me. Therefore go and make disciples of all nations, baptizing them in the name of the Father and of the Son and of the Holy Spirit, and teaching them to obey everything I have commanded you. And surely I am with you always, to the very end of the age" (Matthew 28:18-20).

Believe

Belief in Jesus Christ as your Savior and Lord gives you eternal life in heaven.

> If you declare with your mouth, "Jesus is Lord," and believe in your heart that God raised him from the dead, you will be saved (Romans 10:9).

Repent and be Baptized

To repent is to turn from your sin and then publicly confess Christ in baptism.

> Repent and be baptized, every one of you, in the name of Jesus Christ for the forgiveness of your sins. And you will receive the gift of the Holy Spirit (Acts 2:38).

Obey

Obedience is an indicator of our love for the Lord Jesus and His presence in our life.

> Jesus replied, "Anyone who loves me will obey my teaching. My Father will love them, and we will come to them and make our home with them" (John 14:23).

Worship, Prayer, Community, Evangelism, and Study

Worship and prayer express our gratitude and honor to God and our dependence on His grace. Community and evangelism show our accountability to Christians and compassion for non-Christians. Study to apply the knowledge, understanding, and wisdom of God.

> Every day they continued to meet together in the temple courts. They broke bread in their homes and ate together with glad and sincere hearts, praising God and enjoying the favor of all the people. And the Lord added to their number daily those who were being saved (Acts 2:46-47).

Love God

Intimacy with Almighty God is a growing and loving relationship. We are loved by Him, so we can love others and be empowered by the Holy Spirit to obey His commands.

> Jesus replied: "'Love the Lord your God with all your heart and with all your soul and with all your mind.' This is the first and greatest commandment" (Matthew 22:37-38).

Love People

Our love for others flows from our love for our heavenly Father. We are able to love because He first loved us.

> And the second is like it: "Love your neighbor as yourself" (Matthew 22:39).

Make Disciples

We disciple others because we are grateful to God and to those who disciple us, and we want to obey Christ's last instructions before going to heaven.

> And the things you have heard me say in the presence of many witnesses entrust to reliable people who will also be qualified to teach others (2 Timothy 2:2).

About the Author

Boyd Bailey enjoys the role of chief encouragement officer at Ministry Ventures, a company he cofounded in 1999. His passion is to encourage and equip leaders engaged in kingdom-focused enterprises. Since 2004 he has also served as president and founder of Wisdom Hunters, a ministry that connects people to Christ through devotional writing—with more than 100,000 daily email readers.

Ministry Ventures has trained approximately 1000 faith-based nonprofits and coached for certification more than 200 ministries in the best practices of prayer, board development, ministry model, administration, and fundraising. By God's grace, these ministries have raised more than $100 million, and thousands of people have been led into growing relationships with Jesus Christ.

Prior to Ministry Ventures, Boyd was the national director for Crown Financial Ministries. He was instrumental in the expansion of Crown into 30 major markets across the United States. He was a key facilitator in the $25 million merger between Christian Financial Concepts and Crown Ministries.

Before his work with Crown, Boyd and Andy Stanley started First Baptist Atlanta's north campus, and as an elder, Boyd assisted Andy in the start of North Point Community Church.

Boyd received a bachelor of arts from Jacksonville State University and a masters of divinity from Southwestern Seminary in Fort Worth, Texas. Boyd and his wife, Rita, live in Roswell, Georgia. They have been married 34 years and are blessed with four daughters, three sons-in-law, and five grandchildren.

To learn more about Harvest House books and
to read sample chapters, visit our website:

www.harvesthousepublishers.com

HARVEST HOUSE PUBLISHERS
EUGENE, OREGON